AN

ESSAY

ON THE

LEARNING OF SHAKSPEARE.

ADDRESSED TO

JOSEPH CRADOCK, ESQ.

BY RICHARD FARMER, D.D., *1735-1797,*

Master of Emmanuel College, Cambridge, and Principal Librarian of that
University.

London :

PRINTED FOR **T.** AND H RODD, 17, LITTLE NEWPORT STREET,

LEICESTER SQUARE. 1821.

AMS PRESS, INC.
NEW YORK
1966

AMS PRESS, INC.
New York, N.Y. 10003
1966

This book, including pagination, is a faithful
reproduction of the original edition.

Manufactured in the United States of America

PREFACE

THE SECOND EDITION,

1767.

THE author of the following Essay was solicitous only for the honour of *Shakspeare:* he
hath however, in *his own* capacity, little reason
to complain of *occasional* criticks, or criticks *by
profession.* The very Few, who have been pleased
to controvert any part of his doctrine, have favoured him with better manners than arguments,
and claim his thanks for a further opportunity of
demonstrating the futility of *theoretick* reasoning
against *matter of fact.* It is indeed strange, that
any *real* friends of our immortal Poet should be
still willing to force him into a situation which is
not tenable: treat him as a *learned* man, and
what shall excuse the most gross violations of
history, chronology, and geography?

Οὐ πείσεις, ἠδ' ἢν πείσῃς is the motto of every
polemick: like his brethren at the *amphitheatre,*
he holds it a merit to *die hard;* and will not say,
enough, though the battle be decided. "Were
it shewn (says some one) that the old bard bor-

rowed *all* his allusions from *English* books then
published, our *Essayist* might have possibly esta-
blished his system."—In good time!——This had
scarcely been attempted by *Peter Burman* himself, with the library of *Shakspeare* before him.
—" Truly, (as Mr. *Dogberry* says,) for *mine
own* part, if I were as tedious as a king, I could
find in my heart to bestow it all on this subject:"
but where should I meet with a reader?—When
the main pillars are taken away, the whole build-
ing falls in course: Nothing hath been, or can
be, pointed out, which is not easily removed; or
rather which was not *virtually* removed before:
a very little *analogy* will do the business. I shall
therefore have no occasion to trouble myself any
further; and may venture to call my pamphlet,
in the words of a pleasant declaimer against *ser-
mons on the thirtieth of January*, " an answer to
every thing that shall hereafter be written on the
subject."

But " this method of reasoning will prove
any one ignorant of the languages who hath
written when translations were extant."——*Shade
of Burgersdicius!*—does it follow, because *Shakspeare*'s early life was incompatible with a course
of education—whose contemporaries, friends and
foes, nay, and himself likewise, agree in his want
of what is usually called *literature*—whose mis-
takes from equivocal translations, and even typo-

graphical errors, cannot possibly be accounted
for otherwise,—that *Locke,* to whom not one of
these circumstances is applicable, understood no
Greek?—I suspect *Rollin*'s opinion of our philosopher was not founded on this argument.

Shakspeare wanted not the stilts of languages
to raise him above all other men. The quotation
from *Lilly* in the *Taming of the Shrew,* if indeed it be his, strongly proves the extent of his
reading: had he known *Terence,* he would not
have quoted erroneously from his *Grammar.*
Every one hath met with men in common life,
who, according to the language of the *Water-
poet,* " got only from *possum* to *posset,*" and yet
will throw out a line occasionally from their *Ac-
cidence* or their *Cato de Moribus* with tolerable
propriety.——If, however, the old editions be
trusted in this passage, our author's memory
somewhat failed him in point of *concord.*

The rage of *parallelisms* is almost over, and
in truth nothing can be more absurd. " THIS
was stolen from *one* classick,—THAT from *another;*" and had I not stept in to his rescue, poor
Shakspeare had been stript as naked of ornament,
as when he first *held horses* at the door of the
playhouse.

The late ingenious and modest Mr. *Dodsley*
declared himself

" Untutor'd in the lore of *Greece* or *Rome:*"

yet let us take a passage at a venture from any of his performances, and, a thousand to one, it is stolen. Suppose it be his celebrated compliment to the *ladies,* in one of his earliest pieces, *The Toy-shop:* " A good wife makes the cares of the world sit easy, and adds a sweetness to its pleasures; she is a man's best companion in prosperity, and his only friend in adversity; the carefullest preserver of his health, and the kindest attendant in his sickness; a faithful adviser in distress, a comforter in affliction, and a prudent manager in all his domestick affairs." *Plainly,* from a fragment of *Euripides* preserved by *Stobœus :*

" Γυνὴ γὰρ ἐν κακοῖσι καὶ νόσοις πόσει
" Ἥδιστόν ἐστι, δώματ᾽ ἢν οἰκῇ καλῶς,
" Ὀργήν τε πραΰνουσα, καὶ δυθυμίας
" ψυχὴν μεθιστᾶς᾽ !" —— *Par.* 4to. 1623.

Malvolio, in the *Twelfth Night* of Shakspeare, hath some expressions very similar to *Alnaschar* in the *Arabian Tales;* which perhaps may be sufficient for *some* criticks to prove his acquaintance with *Arabic!*

It seems however, at last, that " *Taste* should determine the matter." This, as *Bardolph* expresses it, is a *word of exceeding good command:* but I am willing that the standard itself be somewhat better ascertained before it be opposed to demonstrative evidence.——Upon the whole, I may consider myself as the *pioneer* of the *com-mentators:* I have removed a deal of *learned rubbish,* and pointed out to them *Shakspeare's* track in the ever-pleasing *paths of nature.* This was necessarily a previous inquiry; and I hope I may assume with some confidence, what one of the first criticks of the age was pleased to declare on reading the former edition, that " The question is *now* for ever decided."

ADVERTISEMENT

PREFIXED TO

THE THIRD EDITION,

1789.

————

IT may be necessary to apologize for the republication of this pamphlet. The fact is, it has been for a good while extremely scarce, and some mercenary publishers were induced by the extravagant price, which it has occasionally borne, to project a new edition without the consent of the author.

A few corrections might probably be made, and many additional proofs of the argument have necessarily occurred in more than twenty years; some of which may be found in the late admirable editions of our Poet, by Mr. *Steevens* and Mr. *Reed*.

But, perhaps enough is already said on so light a subject;—a subject, however, which had for a long time pretty warmly divided the criticks upon *Shakspeare*.

ESSAY

LEARNING OF SHAKSPEARE.

—

Addressed to JOSEPH CRADOCK, *Esq.*

———

" SHAKSPEARE," says a brother of the *craft**, " is a vast garden of criticism:" and certainly no one can be favoured with more weeders *gratis*.

But how often, my dear sir, are weeds and flowers torn up indiscriminately?—the ravaged spot is replanted in a moment, and a profusion of critical thorns thrown over it for security.

" A prudent man, therefore, would not venture his fingers amongst them."

Be however in little pain for your friend, who regards himself sufficiently to be cautious:—yet he asserts with confidence, that no improvement can be expected, whilst the natural soil is mistaken for a hot-bed, and the natives of the banks of *Avon*

———

* Mr. Seward, in his Preface to *Beaumont and Fletcher.* 10 vols. 8vo, 1750.

are scientifically choked with the culture of ex-
oticks.

Thus much for metaphor; it is contrary to the
statute to fly out so early: but who can tell,
whether it may not be demonstrated by some
critick or other, that a deviation from rule is peculiarly happy in an *Essay on Shakspeare ?*

You have long known my opinion concerning
the literary acquisitions of our immortal dra-
matist, and remember how I congratulated myself on my coincidence with the last and best of
his editors. I told you, however, that his *small
Latin and less Greek** would still be litigated, and
you see very assuredly that I was not mistaken.
The trumpet hath been sounded against "the
darling project of representing Shakspeare as one
of the illiterate vulgar;" and indeed to so good
purpose, that I would by all means recommend
the performer to the army of the *braying faction*,
recorded by *Cervantes*. The testimony of his
contemporaries is again disputed; constant tradition is opposed by flimsy arguments; and nothing

---

* This passage of *Ben Jonson,* so often quoted, is given
us in the admirable preface to the late edition, with a various reading, " small Latin and *no* Greek," which hath
been held up to the publick for a modern sophistication:
yet whether an error or not, it was adopted above a century ago by *W. Towers,* in a panegyrick on *Cartwright.*
His Eulogy, with more than fifty others, on this now forgotten poet, was prefixed to the edit. 1651.

is heard, but confusion and nonsense. One could scarcely imagine this a topick very likely to inflame the passions: it is asserted by Dryden, that "those who accuse him to have wanted learning, give him the greatest commendation;" yet an attack upon an article of faith hath been usually received with more temper and complacence, than the unfortunate opinion which I am about to defend.

But let us previously lament with every lover of Shakspeare that the question was not fully discussed by Mr. Johnson himself: what he sees intuitively, others must arrive at by a series of proofs; and I have not time to *teach* with precision: be contented therefore with a few cursory observations, as they may happen to arise from the chaos of papers you have so often laughed at, " a stock sufficient to set up an *editor in form*." I am convinced of the strength of my cause, and superior to any little advantage from sophistical arrangements.

General positions without proofs will probably have no great weight on either side, yet it may not seem fair to suppress them: take them therefore as their authors occur to me, and we will afterward proceed to particulars.

The testimony of Ben stands foremost; and some have held it sufficient to decide the controversy: in the warmest panegyrick that ever was

C

written, he apologizes* for what *he* supposed the
only defect in his " beloved friend,—

   ' ———— Soul of the age!
   ' Th' applause ! delight ! the wonder of our stage!'—

whose memory he honoured almost to idolatry :"
and conscious of the worth of ancient literature, like
any other man on the same occasion, he rather
carries his acquirements *above* than *below* the truth.
"Jealousy!" cries Mr. Upton; "people will allow
others any qualities, but those upon which they
highly value *themselves*." Yes, where there *is*
a competition, and the competitor formidable :
but, I think, this critick himself hath scarcely
set in opposition the learning of Shakspeare and
Jonson. When a superiority is universally granted,
it by no means appears a man's literary interest
to depress the reputation of his antagonist.

   In truth, the received opinion of the pride and
malignity of Jonson, at least in the earlier part
of life, is absolutely groundless : at this time
scarce a play or a poem appeared without Ben's
encomium, from the original Shakspeare to the
translator of Du Bartas.

   But Jonson is by no means our only authority.
Drayton, the countryman and acquaintance of
Shakspeare, determines his excellence to the
naturall braine† only. Digges, a wit of the

---

   * " *Though* thou hadst *small Latin*," &c.
   † In his *Elegie on Poets and Poesie*, p. 206. Folio, 1627.

town before our poet left the stage, is very strong
to the purpose :

" —— Nature only helpt him, for looke thorow
" This whole book, thou shalt find he doth not borow;
" One phrase from Greekes, not Latines imitate,
" Nor once from vulgar languages translate*".

Suckling opposed his *easier strain* to the *sweat
of the learned Jonson*. Denham assures us, that
all he had was from *old mother-wit*. *His native
wood-notes wild*, every one remembers to be celebrated by Milton. Dryden observes prettily
enough, that " he wanted not the spectacles of
books to read nature." He came out of her hand,
as some one else expresses it, like *Pallas* out of
Jove's head, at full growth and mature.

The ever memorable Hales of Eton (who,
notwithstanding his epithet, is, I fear, almost forgotten) had too great a knowledge both of
Shakspeare and the ancients to allow much acquaintance between them ; and urged very justly
on the part of genius in opposition to pedantry,
that " if he had not *read* the classicks, he had
likewise not *stolen* from them ; and if any topick

* From his *Poem upon Master William Shakspeare*, intended to have been prefixed, with the other of his composition, to the folio of 1623, and afterward printed in
several miscellaneous collections; particularly the spurious
edition of *Shakspeare's Poems*, 1640. Some account of
him may be met with in *Wood's Athenæ*.

was produced from a poet of antiquity, he would undertake to show somewhat on the same subject, at least, as well written by Shakspeare."

Fuller, a diligent and equal searcher after truth and quibbles, declares positively, that "his learning was very little,—*nature* was all the *art* used upon him, as *he himself*, if alive, would confess." And may we not say, he did confess it, when he apologized for his *untutored lines* to his noble patron the Earl of Southampton?—This list of witnesses might be easily enlarged; but I flatter myself I shall stand in no need of such evidence.

One of the first and most vehement assertors of the learning of Shakspeare, was the editor of his poems, the well-known Mr. Gildon*; and his steps were most punctually taken by a subsequent labourer in the same department, Dr. Sewell.

* Hence perhaps the *ill-starr'd rage* between this critick and his elder brother, John Dennis, so pathetically lamented in the *Dunciad*. Whilst the former was persuaded that " the man who doubts of the learning of Shakspeare hath none of his own," the latter, above regarding the attack in his *private* capacity, declares with great patriotick vehemence, that " he who allows Shakspeare had learning, and a familiar acquaintance with the ancients, ought to be looked upon as a detractor from the glory of Great Britain." Dennis was expelled his college for attempting to stab a man in the dark: Pope would have been glad of this anecdote.

Mr. Pope supposed " little ground for the common opinion of his want of learning :" once indeed he made a proper distinction between *learning* and *languages,* as I would be understood to do in my title-page; but unfortunately he forgot it in the course of his disquisition, and endeavoured to persuade himself that Shakspeare's acquaintance with the ancients might be actually proved by the same medium as Jonson's.

Mr. Theobald is " very unwilling' to allow him so poor a scholar, as many have laboured to represent him ;" and yet is " cautious of declaring too positively on the other side of the question."

Dr. Warburton hath exposed the weakness of some arguments from *suspected* imitations ; and yet offers others, which, I doubt not, he could as easily have refuted.

Mr. Upton wonders " with what kind of reasoning any one could be so far imposed upon, as to imagine that Shakspeare had no learning ;" and lashes with much zeal and satisfaction " the pride and pertness of dunces, who, under such a name, would gladly shelter their own idleness and ignorance."

He, like the learned knight, at every anomaly in grammar or metre,

> " Hath hard words ready to show why,
> " And tell what *rule* he did it by."

How would the old bard have been astonished to have found, that he had very skilfully given the *trochaic dimeter brachycatalectic*, COMMONLY called the *ithyphallic* measure to the Witches in *Macbeth!* and that now and then a halting verse afforded a most beautiful instance of the *pes proceleusmaticus!*

" But," continues Mr. Upton, " it was a learned age; Roger Ascham assures us, that Queen Elizabeth read more Greek every day, than some *dignitaries* of the church did Latin in a whole week." This appears very probable; and a pleasant proof it is of the general learning of the times, and of Shakspeare in particular. I wonder he did not corroborate it with an extract from her injunctions to her clergy, that " such as were but *mean readers* should peruse over before, once or twice, the chapters and homilies, to the intent they might read to the better understanding of the people."

Dr. Grey declares, that Shakspeare's knowledge in the Greek and Latin tongues cannot *reasonably* be called in question. Dr. Dodd supposes it proved, that he was not such a novice in learning and antiquity as *some people* would pretend. And to close the whole, for I suspect you to be tired of quotation, Mr. Whalley, the ingenious editor of Jonson, hath written a piece expressly on this side the question: perhaps, from a very excusable partiality, he was willing to draw Shakspeare from the field of nature to classick ground, where alone, he knew, his author could possibly cope with him.

These criticks, and many others their coadjutors, have supposed themselves able to trace Shakspeare in the writings of the ancients, and have sometimes persuaded us of their own learning, whatever became of their author's. Plagiarisms have been discovered in every natural description and every moral sentiment. Indeed, by the kind assistance of the various *Excerpta, Sententiæ,* and *Flores,* this business may be effected with very little expence of time or sagacity; as Addison hath demonstrated in his comment on *Chevy-chase,* and Wagstaff on *Tom Thumb;* and I myself will engage to give you quotations from the elder English writers (for, to own the truth I was once idle enough to collect such) which shall carry with them at least an equal degree of similarity. But there can be no occasion of wasting any future time in this department: the world is now in possession of the *Marks of Imitation.*

" Shakspeare however hath frequent allusions to the *facts* and *fables* of antiquity." Granted: —and as Mat. Prior says, to save the effusion of more Christian ink, I will endeavour to show how they came to his acquaintance.

It is notorious, that much of his *matter of fact* knowledge is deduced from Plutarch : but in what language he read him hath yet been the question. Mr. Upton is pretty confident of his skill in the original, and corrects accordingly the *errors of his copyists* by the Greek standard. Take a few instances, which will elucidate this matter sufficiently.

In the third act of *Antony and Cleopatra,* Octavius represents to his courtiers the imperial pomp of those illustrious lovers, and the arrangement of their dominion :

  " ———————————————— Unto her
  " He gave the 'stablishment of Egypt, made her
  " Of lower Syria, Cyprus, *Lydia,*
  " Absolute queen."

Read *Libya,* says the critick *authoritatively,* as is plain from *Plutarch,* Πρώτην μὲν ἀπέφηνε Κλεοπάτραν βασίλισσαν Αἰγύπτε καὶ Κύπρε καὶ ΛΙΒΥΗΣ, καὶ κοίλης Συρίας.

This is very true : Mr. Heath* accedes to the correction, and Mr. Johnson admits it into the text: but turn to the translation, from the French

————————————————
* It is extraordinary, that this gentleman should attempt so voluminous a work as the *Revisal of Shakspeare's Text,* when he tells us in his Preface " he was not so fortunate as to be furnished with either of the *folio* editions, much less any of the ancient *quartos:*" and even "Sir Thomas Hanmer's performance was known to him only by Mr. Warburton's representation."

of Amyot, by Thomas North, in folio, 1579*, and you will at once see the origin of the mistake.

" First of all he did establish Cleopatra queene of Ægypt, of Cyprus, of *Lidya*, and the lower Syria."

Again, in the fourth act:

" ——————————— My messenger
" He hath whipt with rods, dares me to personal combat,
" Cæsar to Antony. Let th' old ruffian know
" I have many other ways to die; mean time
" Laugh at his challenge.———"

" What a reply is this!" cries Mr. Upton: " 'tis acknowledging he should fall under the unequal combat. But if we read,

' ——— Let th' old ruffian know
' *He* hath many other ways to die; mean time
' *I* laugh at his challenge,———'

we have the poignancy and the very repartee of Cæsar in Plutarch."

This correction was first made by Sir Thomas Hanmer, and Mr. Johnson hath received it. Most indisputably it is the sense of Plutarch, and given so in the modern translations: but Shakspeare

---

* I find the character of this work pretty early delineated:
" 'Twas Greek at first, that Greek was Latin made,
" That Latin French; that French to English straid:
" Thus 'twixt one Plutarch there's more difference,
" Than i' th' same Englishman return'd from France."

D

was misled by the ambiguity of the old one:
" Antonius sent again to challenge Cæsar to
fight him : Cæsar answered, That *he* had many
other ways to die, than so."

In the third act of *Julius Cæsar,* Antony, in
his well-known harangue to the people, repeats a
part of the emperor's will :

> " —— To every Roman citizen he gives,
> " To every sev'ral man, seventy-five drachmas.——
> " Moreover he hath left you all his walks,
> " His private arbours, and new-planted orchards,
> " On *this* side Tiber.——"

" Our author certainly wrote," says Mr. Theobald,— " On *that* side Tiber—

> ' *Trans* Tiberim—prope Cæsaris hortos.'

And Plutarch, whom Shakspeare very diligently
studied, expressly declares, that he left the publick
his gardens and walks, πέραν τȣ̃ Ποταμȣ̃, *beyond* the
Tyber."

This emendation likewise hath been adopted
by the subsequent Editors; but hear again the
old Translation, where *Shakspeare's study* lay,
" He bequeathed unto every citizen of Rome
seventy-five drachmas a man, and he left his gardens and arbours unto the people, which he had
on *this* side of the river of Tyber." I could fur-
nish you with many more instances, but these are
as good as a thousand.

Hence had our author his characteristick know-ledge of *Brutus* and *Antony,* upon which much argumentation for his learning hath been founded: and hence *literatim* the Epitaph on *Timon,* which it was once presumed he had corrected from the blunders of the Latin version, by his own supe-rior knowledge of the Original*.

I cannot however omit a passage of Mr. *Pope.* " The *speeches* copy'd from *Plutarch* in *Coriola-nus* may, I think, be as well made an instance of the learning of *Shakspeare,* as those copy'd from *Cicero* in *Catiline,* of *Ben Jonson's.*" Let us inquire into this matter, and transcribe a *speech* for a specimen. Take the famous one of *Vo-lumnia :*

> " Should we be silent and not speak, our raiment
> And state of bodies would bewray what life
> We've led since thy Exile.   Think with thyself,
> How more unfortunate than all living women
> Are we come hither ; since thy sight, which should
> Make our eyes flow with joy, hearts dance with comforts,
> Constrains them weep, and shake with fear and sorrow:
> Making the mother, wife, and child to see
> The son, the husband, and the father tearing
> His Country's bowels out : and to poor we
> Thy enmity's most capital ; thou barr'st us
> Our prayers to the Gods, which is a comfort
> That all but we enjoy.   For how can we,
> Alas ! how can we, for our Country pray,

---

* See *Theobald*'s Preface to K. *Richard* II, 8vo. 1720.

Whereto we're bound, together with thy Victory,
Whereto we're bound? Alack! or we must lose
The Country, our dear nurse; or else thy person,
Our comfort in the country.   We must find
An eminent calamity, though we had
Our wish, which side shou'd win.   For either thou
Must, as a foreign Recreant, be led
With manacles thorough our streets; or else
Triumphantly tread on thy Country's ruin,
And bear the palm, for having bravely shed
Thy wife and children's blood.   For myself, son,
I purpose not to wait on Fortune, till
These wars determine: if I can't persuade thee
Rather to shew a noble grace to both parts
Than seek the end of one, thou shalt no sooner
March to assault thy Country, than to tread
(Trust to't, thou shalt not) on thy mother's womb,
That brought thee to this world."

I will now give you the old Translation, which
shall effectually confute Mr. *Pope;* for our
Author hath done little more, than thrown the
very words of *North* into blank verse.

" If we helde our peace (my sonne) and determined not to speake, the state of our poore
bodies, and present sight of our rayment, would
easely bewray to thee what life we haue led at
home, since thy exile and abode abroad.   But
thinke now with thy selfe, howe much more
unfortunately then all the women liuinge we are
come hether, considering that 'the sight which
should be most pleasaunt to all other to beholde,

spitefull fortune hath made most fearfull to us:
making my selfe to see my sonne, and my
daughter here, her husband, besieging the walles
of his natiue countrie. So as that which is the
only comfort to all other in their adversitie and
miserie, to pray unto the goddes, and to call to
them for aide; is the onely thinge which plongeth
us into most deepe perplexitie. For we cannot
(alas) together pray, both for victorie, for our
countrie, and for safety of thy life also: but a
worlde of grievous curses, yea more than any
mortall enemie can heappe uppon us, are forcibly
wrapt up in our prayers. For the bitter soppe of
most harde choyce is offered thy wife and
children, to foregoe the one of the two: either to
lose the persone of thy selfe, or the nurse of
their natiue contrie. For my selfe (my sonne)
I am determined not to tarrie, till fortune in my
life time doe make an ende of this warre. For
if I cannot persuade thee, rather to doe good
unto both parties, then to ouerthrowe and destroye
the one, preferring loue and nature before the
malice and calamitie of warres: thou shalt see,
my sonne, and trust unto it, thou shalt no soner
marche forward to assault thy countrie, but thy
foote shall tread upon thy mother's wombe, that
brought thee first into this world."

The length of this quotation will be excused
for its curiosity; and it happily wants not the

assistance of a Comment. But matters may not always be so easily managed :—a plagiarism from *Anacreon* hath been detected.

> " The Sun's a thief, and with his great attraction
> Robs the vast Sea. The Moon's an arrant thief,
> And her pale fire she snatches from the Sun.
> The Sea's a thief, whose liquid surge resolves
> The Moon into salt tears. The Earth's a thief,
> That feeds and breeds by a composture stol'n
> From gen'ral excrements : each thing's a thief."

" This, says Dr. *Dodd,* is a good deal in the manner of the celebrated *drinking Ode,* too well known to be inserted." Yet it may be alleged by those, who imagine *Shakspeare* to have been generally able to think for himself, that the topicks are obvious, and their application is different.—But, for argument's sake, let the Parody be granted : and " our Author, says some one, may be puzzled to prove, that there was a *Latin* translation of *Anacreon* at the time *Shakspeare* wrote his *Timon of Athens.*" This challenge is peculiarly unhappy : for I do not at present recollect any *other Classick* (if indeed, with great deference to *Mynheer De Pauw, Anacreon* may be numbered amongst them) that was *originally* published with *two Latin** translations.

* By *Henry Stephens* and *Elias Andreas, Par.* 1554, 4to, ten years before the birth of *Shakspeare.* The former Version hath been ascribed without reason to *John Dorat.*

But this is not all. *Puttenham*, in his *Arte of English Poesie*, 1589, quotes some one of a " reasonable good facilitie in translation, who finding *certaine* of *Anacreon's* Odes very well translated by *Ronsard* the French poet, comes our minion, and translates the same out of *French* into *English :*" and his strictures upon him evince the publication. Now this identical Ode is to be met with in *Ronsard!* and as his works are in few hands, I will take the liberty of transcribing it.

> " La terre les eaux va boivant,
> L'arbre la boit par sa racine,
> La mer salee boit le vent,
> Et le Soleil boit la marine.
> Le Soleil est beu de la Lune,
> Tout boit soit en haut ou en bas :
> Suivant ceste reigle commune,
> Pourquoy donc ne boirons-nous pas?"
>
> Edit. Fol. p. 507.

I know not whether an observation or two relative to our Author's acquaintance with *Homer* be worth our investigation. The ingenious Mrs. *Lenox* observes on a passage of *Troilus and Cressida*, where *Achilles* is roused to battle by

---

Many other Translators appeared before the end of the century: and particularly the Ode in question was made popular by *Buchanan*, whose pieces were soon to be met with in almost every modern language.

the death of *Patroclus*, that *Shakspeare* must *here* have had the *Iliad* in view, as "the old Story*, which in many places he hath faithfully copied, is absolutely silent with respect to this circumstance."

And Mr. *Upton* is positive that the *sweet oblivious Antidote*, inquired after by *Macbeth*, could be nothing but the *Nepenthe* described in the *Odyssey*,

" Νηπενθές τ᾽ ἀχολόν τε, κακῶν ἐπίληθον ἀπάντων."

I will not insist upon the Translations by *Chapman*, as the first Editions are without date, and it may be difficult to ascertain the exact time of their publication. But the *former* circumstance might have been learned from *Alexander Barclay†*; and the *latter* more fully from *Spenser‡*, than from *Homer* himself.

---

* It was originally *drawn into Englishe* by *Caxton*, under the name of the *Recuyel of the Historyes of Troy*, from the *French* of the *ryght venerable Person and worshipfull man Raoul le Feure*, and *fynyshed in the holy citye of Colen, the 19 day of Septembre, the yere of our Lord God, a thousand foure hundred sixty and enleuen. Wynken de Worde* printed an Edit. Fol. 1503; and there have been several subsequent ones.

† " Who list thistory of *Patroclus* to reade, &c."
             Ship of Fooles, 1570, p. 21.

‡ " Nepenthe is a drinck of soueragne grace,
    Deuized by the Gods, for to asswage
Harts grief, and bitter gall away to chace——
    Instead thereof sweet peace and quietage
It doth establish in the troubled mynd, &c."
             Faerie Queene, 1596. B. 4, C. 3, St. 43.

" But *Shakspeare*," persists Mr. *Upton*, "hath some *Greek Expressions*."   Indeed!—" We have one in *Coriolanus*,

—————————— ———— " It is held
That valour is the chiefest Virtue, and
Most dignifies the *Haver*."——

and another in *Macbeth*, where *Banquo* addresses the *Weïrd-Sisters*,

————— ——————— " My noble Partner
You greet with present grace, and great prediction
Of noble *Having*."

Gr. "Εχμα.—and πρὸς τὸν "Εχοντα, to the *Haver*."
This was the common language of *Shakspeare*'s time. " Lye in a water-bearer's house!" says Master *Mathew* of *Bobadil*, " a Gentleman of his *Havings!*"

Thus likewise *John Davies* in his *Pleasant Descant upon English Proverbs*, printed with his *Scourge of Folly*, about 1612;

" *Do well and have well!*—neyther so still :
For some are good *Doers* whose *Havings* are ill."

and *Daniel* the Historian uses it frequently. *Having* seems to be synonymous with *Behaviour* in *Gawin Douglas** and the elder Scotch writers.

* It is very remarkable, that the Bishop is called by his Countryman, Sir *David Lindsey*, in his *Complaint of our Souerane Lordis Papingo*,

" In *our Inglische* Rethorick the Rose :"

E

Haver, in the sense of *Possessor,* is every where met with; tho' unfortunately the πρὸς τὸν Ἔχοντα of *Sophocles,* produced as an authority for it, is suspected by *Kuster*,* as good a critick in these matters, to have absolutely a different meaning.

But what shall we say to the learning of the *Clown* in *Hamlet,* "Ay, tell me that, and *unyoke?*" alluding to the Βωλτὸς of the *Greeks:* and *Homer* and his Scholiast are quoted accordingly!

If it be not sufficient to say, with Dr. *Warburton,* that the phrase might be taken from Husbandry, without much depth of reading; we may produce it from a *Dittie* of the workmen of *Dover,* preserved in the additions to *Holingshed,* p. 1546.

> "My bow is broke, I would *unyoke;*
> My foot is sore, I can worke no more."

An expression of my Dame *Quickly* is next fastened upon, which you may look for in vain in the modern text; she calls some of the pretended Fairies in the *Merry Wives of Windsor,*

——— "*Orphan*† Heirs of fixed Destiny."

and *Dunbar* hath a similar expression in his beautiful Poem of *The Goldin Terge.*

* *Aristophanis* Comœdiæ undecim. Gr. & Lat. *Amst.* 1710. Fol. p. 596.

† Dr. *Warburton* corrects *Orphan* to *Ouphen;* and not

" and how elegant is this," quoth Mr. *Upton,* supposing the word to be used, as a *Grecian* would
have used it ? " ὀξφανὸς ab ὀξφνὸς—acting in darkness
and obscurity."

Mr. *Heath* assures us, that the bare mention
of such an interpretation is a sufficient refutation
of it : and his critical word will be rather taken
in *Greek* than in *English :* in the same hands
therefore I will venture to leave all our author's
knowledge of the *Old Comedy,* and his etymolo-
gical learning in the word *Desdemona*.*

Surely poor Mr. *Upton* was very little acquainted with *Fairies,* notwithstanding his laborious study of *Spenser.* The last authentick ac-

without plausibility, as the word *Ouphes* occurs both
before and afterward.   But I fancy, in acquiescence to the
vulgar doctrine, the address in this line is to a part of the
Troop, as Mortals by birth, but adopted by the Fairies ;
Orphans, with respect to their *real* Parents, and now only
dependant on *Destiny* herself.   A few lines from *Spenser*
will sufficiently illustrate the passage :

> " The man whom *heauens* have *ordaynd* to bee
>   The spouse of *Britomart,* is *Arthegall :*
> He wonneth in the land of *Fayeree,*
>   Yet is no *Fary* borne, ne sib at all
> To Elfes, but sprong of seed terrestriall,
>   And whilome by false *Faries* stolen away,
> Whyles yet in infant cradle he did crall, &c."
>   Edit. 1590, B. 3, C. 3, St. 26.

* *Revisal,* p. 75, 323, & 561.

count of them is from our countryman *William Lilly**; and it by no means agrees with the *learned* interpretation: for the *angelical Creatures* appeared in his *Hurst* wood in a *most illustrious Glory*,—" and indeed, says the Sage, it is not given to very many persons to endure their *glorious aspects.*"

The only use of transcribing these things, is to shew what absurdities men for ever run into, when they lay down an hypothesis, and afterward seek for arguments in the support of it. What else could induce this man, by no means a bad scholar, to doubt whether *Truepenny* might not be derived from Τρύπανον; and quote upon us with much parade an old scholiast on *Aristophanes ?*— I will not stop to confute him; nor take any notice of two or three more expressions, in which he was pleased to suppose some learned meaning or other; all which he might have found in every Writer of the time, or still more easily in the vulgar Translation of the Bible, by consulting the Concordance of *Alexander Cruden.*

But whence have we the Plot of *Timon,* except from the *Greek* of *Lucian ?*—The Editors and Criticks have been never at a greater loss than in their inquiries of this sort; and the source of a Tale hath been often in vain sought

* History of his Life and Times, p. 102, preserved by his dupe, Mr. *Ashmole.*

abroad, which might easily have been found at home: My good friend, the very ingenious Editor of the *Reliques of ancient English Poetry,* hath shewn our Author to have been sometimes contented with a legendary *Ballad.*

The Story of the *Misanthrope* is told in almost every collection of the time ; and particularly in two books, with which *Shakspeare* was intimately acquainted,—the *Palace of Pleasure,* and the *English Plutarch.* Indeed from a passage in an old Play, called *Jack Drums Entertainment,* I conjecture that he had before made his appearance on the Stage.

Were this a proper place for such a disquisition, I could give you many cases of this kind. We are sent for instance to *Cinthio* for the Plot of *Measure for Measure,* and *Shakspeare*'s judgement hath been attacked for some deviations from him in the conduct of it ; when probably all he knew of the matter was from Madam *Isabella* in the *Heptameron* of *Whetstone*.* *Ariosto* is continually quoted for the Fable of *Much ado about Nothing ;* but I suspect our Poet to have been satisfied with the *Geneura* of *Turberville†.*

* Lond. 4to. 1582. She *reports* in the fourth dayes exercise, the rare *Historie* of *Promos and Cassandra.* A marginal note informs us, that *Whetstone* was the Author of the *Commedie* on that subject ; which likewise might have fallen into the hands of *Shakspeare.*

† " The tale is a pretie comicall matter, and hath bin

As you like it was *certainly borrowed,* if we
believe **Dr.** *Grey* and **Mr.** *Upton,* from the *Coke's
Tale of Gamelyn,* which by the way was not
printed till a century afterward ; when in truth
the old Bard, who was no hunter of MSS. contented himself solely with *Lodge*'s *Rosalynd* or
Euphues' Golden Legacye, 4to, 1590. The
Story of *All's well that ends well,* or, as I suppose it to have been sometimes called, *Love's
labour wonne*,* is originally indeed the property
of *Boccace†,* but it came immediately to *Shaks-*

written in *English* verse some few years past, learnedly
and with good grace, by M. *George Turberuil."* *Harrington's Ariosto,* Fol. 1591, p. 39.

* See *Meres's Wits Treasury,* 1598, p. 282.

† Our ancient Poets are under greater obligations to
Boccace than is generally imagined. Who would suspect,
that *Chaucer* hath borrowed from an *Italian* the facetious
Tale of the *Miller of Trumpington?*

Mr. *Dryden* observes on the Epic performance, *Palamon
and Arcite,* a poem little inferior in his opinion to the *Iliad*
or the *Æneid,* that the name of its Author is wholly lost, and
Chaucer is now become the Original. But he is mistaken :
this too was the work of *Boccace,* and printed at *Ferrara* in
Folio, *con il commento di Andrea Bassi,* 1475. I have seen
a copy of it, and a Translation into modern *Greek,* in the
noble library of the very learned and communicative Dr.
Askew.

It is likewise to be met with in old *French,* under the Title
of *La Theseide* de *Jean Boccace,* contenant les belles &
chastes amours de deux jeunes Chevaliers Thebains *Arcite
& Palemon.*

peare from *Painter's Giletta* of *Narbon**. Mr. *Langbaine* could not conceive whence the Story of *Pericles* could be taken, " not meeting in History with any such *Prince of Tyre;*" yet his legend may be found at large in old *Gower,* under the name of *Appolynus*†.

Pericles is one of the Plays omitted in the later Editions, as well as the early Folios, and not improperly; tho' it was published many years before the death of *Shakspeare,* with his name in the Title-page. *Aulus Gellius* informs us, that some Plays are ascribed absolutely to *Plautus* which he only *retouched* and *polished;* and this is undoubtedly the case with our Author likewise. The revival of this performance, which *Ben Jonson* calls *stale* and *mouldy,* was probably his earliest attempt in the Drama. I know that another of these discarded pieces, the *Yorkshire Tragedy,* hath been frequently called so ; but most certainly it was not written by our Poet at all, nor indeed was it printed in his life-time. The fact on which it is built was perpetrated no sooner than 1604‡; much too late for so mean a performance from the hand of *Shakspeare.*

---

* In the first Vol. of the *Palace of Pleasure,* 4to. 1566.

† *Confesso Amantis,* printed by *T. Berthelet,* Fol. 1532, p. 176, &c.

‡ " *William Caluerley,* of *Caluerley* in *Yorkshire,* Esquire, murdered two of his owne children in his owne house, then

Sometimes a very little matter detects a forgery. You may remember a Play called the *Double Falshood*, which Mr. *Theobald* was desirous of palming upon the world for a posthumous one of *Shakspeare;* and I see it is classed as such in the last Edition of the *Bodleian* Catalogue. Mr. *Pope* himself, after all the strictures of *Scriblerus**, in a Letter to *Aaron Hill*, supposes it of that age; but a mistaken accent determines it to have been written since the middle of the last century.

> ———————————— " This late example
> Of base Henriquez, bleeding in me now,
> From each good *áspect* takes away my trust."

And in another place,

> " You have an *áspect*, Sir, of wondrous wisdom."

The word *Aspect*, you perceive, is here accented on the *first* Syllable, which, I am confident, in *any* sense of it, was never the case in

---

stabde his wife into the body with full intent to haue killed her, and then instantlie with like fury went from his house, to haue slaine his yongest childe at nurse, but was preuented. Hee was prest to death in *Yorke* the 5 of *August*, 1604." *Edm. Howes'* Continuation of *John Stowe's* Summarie, 8vo, 1607, p. 574. The Story appeared before in a 4to pamphlet, 1605 : it is omitted in the *Folio* Chronicle, 1631.

＊ These, however, he assures Mr. *Hill*, were the property of Dr. *Arbuthnot*.

the time of *Shakspeare;* though it may sometimes appear to be so, when we do not observe a
preceding *Elision**.

Some of the professed Imitators of our old
Poets have not attended to this and many other
Minutiæ : I could point out to you several per-
formances in the respective *styles* of *Chaucer,
Spenser,* and *Shakspeare,* which the *imitated* Bard
could not possibly have either read or construed.

This very accent hath troubled the Annotators
on *Milton.* Dr. *Bentley* observes it to be " a
tone different from the present use." Mr. *Man-
waring,* in his *Treatise of Harmony and Num-
bers,* very solemnly informs us, that " this Verse
is defective both in Accent and Quantity, b. 3,
v. 266.

> " His words here ended, but his meek *aspéct*
> Silent yet spake."——

Here, says he, a syllable is *acuted* and *long,*
whereas it should be *short* and *graved!"*

And a still more extraordinary Gentleman, one
Green, ʷʰo published a Specimen of a *new Version* of the *Paradise Lost,* into BLANK verse,
" by which that amazing Work is brought some-

---

* Thus a line in *Hamlet*'s description of the *Player*
should be printed as in the old Folios,
" Tears in his eyes, distraction in's aspéct,"
agreeably to the accent in a hundred other places.

F

what nearer the Summit of Perfection," begins
with correcting a blunder in the fourth book,
v. 540 :

> —————— " The sétting Sun
> Slowly descended, and with right *aspéct*—
> Levell'd his evening rays."

Not so in the *New Version* :

> " Meanwhile the setting Sun descending slow—
> Level'd with *áspect* right his ev'ning rays."

Enough of such Commentators.——The celebrated Dr. *Dee* had a *Spirit*, who would sometimes condescend to correct him, when peccant
in *Quantity ;* and it had been kind of him to
have a little assisted the *Wights* abovementioned.
——*Milton* affected the *Antique ;* but it may
seem more extraordinary that the old Accent
should be adopted in *Hudibras*.

After all, the *Double Falshood* is superior to
Theobald. One passage, and one only in the
whole Play, he pretended to have written :

> ——————— " Strike up, my Masters ;
> " But touch the Strings with a religious softness :
> " Teach sound to languish thro' the Night's dull Ear,
> " Till Melancholy start from her lazy Couch,
> " And Carelessness grow Convert to Attention."

These lines were particularly admired ; and his
vanity could not resist the opportunity of claim-

ing them: but his claim had been more easily allowed to *any other* part of the performance.

To whom then shall we ascribe it?—Somebody hath told us, who should seem to a *Nostrum-monger* by his argument, that, let *Accents* be how they will, it is called *an original Play of William Shakspeare* in the *King's Patent,* prefixed to Mr. *Theobald's* Edition, 1728, and consequently there *could* be no fraud in the matter. Whilst, on the contrary, the *Irish* Laureat, Mr. *Victor,* remarks, (and were it true, it would be certainly decisive) that the Plot is borrowed from a Novel of *Cervantes,* not published till the year after *Shakspeare's* death. But unluckily the same Novel appears in a part of *Don Quixote,* which was printed in *Spanish,* 1605, and in *English* by *Shelton,* 1612.——The same reasoning, however, which exculpated our Author from the *Yorkshire Tragedy,* may be applied on the present occasion.

But you want *my* opinion:—and from every mark of Style and Manner, I make no doubt of ascribing it to *Shirley.* Mr. *Langbaine* informs us, that he left some Plays in MS. These were written about the time of the *Restoration,* when the *Accent* in question was more generally altered.

Perhaps the mistake arose from an *abbreviation* of the name. Mr. *Dodsley* knew not

that the Tragedy of *Andromana* was *Shirley's,*
from the very same cause. Thus a whole
stream of Biographers tell us, that *Mars-*
ton's Plays were printed at *London,* 1633, " by
the care of *William Shakspeare,* the famous
Comedian."—Here again I suppose, in some
Transcript, the real Publisher's name, *William*
Sheares, was *abbreviated.* No one hath pro-
tracted the life of *Shakspeare* beyond 1616, except Mr. *Hume;* who is pleased to add a year
to it, in contradiction to all manner of evidence.

Shirley is spoken of with contempt in *Mac*
Flecknoe; but his Imagination is sometimes fine
to an extraordinary degree. I recollect a passage
in the fourth book of the *Paradise Lost,* which
hath been suspected of *Imitation,* as a *prettiness*
below the Genius of *Milton;* I mean, where
Uriel glides *backward and forward* to Heaven on
a *Sun-beam.* Dr. *Newton* informs us, that this
might possibly be hinted by a Picture of *Annibal*
Caracci in the King of *France*'s Cabinet: but I
am apt to believe that *Milton* had been struck
with a Portrait in *Shirley.* *Fernando,* in the
Comedy of the *Brothers,* 1652, describes *Jacinta*
at *Vespers :*

" Her eye did seem to labour with a tear,
 Which suddenly took birth, but overweigh'd
 With it's own swelling, drop'd upon her bosome;
 Which by reflection of her light, appear'd
 As nature meant her sorrow for an ornament :

After, her looks grew chearfull, and I saw
A smile shoot gracefull upward from her eyes,
As if they had gain'd a victory o'er grief,
And with it many *beams* twisted themselves,
Upon whose *golden threads* the *Angels* walk
To and again from Heaven.*" ——

You must not think me infected with the spirit of *Lauder*, if I give you another of *Milton*'s Imitations :

——————— " The Swan *with arched neck*
" Between her white wings mantling proudly, rows
" Her state with oary feet."—B. 7, v. 438, &c.

" The ancient Poets, says Mr. *Richardson*, have not hit upon this beauty ; so lavish as they have been in their descriptions of the *Swan*. *Homer* calls the Swan *long-necked*, δυλιχοδειρον ; but how much more *pittoresque*, if he had *arched* this length of neck ?"

For *this beauty*, however, *Milton* was beholden to *Donne* ; whose name, I believe, at present is better known than his writings :

——————— "Like a Ship in her full trim,
A *Swan*, so white that you may unto him

* *Middleton* in an obscure Play, called, *A Game at Chesse*, hath some very pleasing lines on a similar occasion :
" Upon those lips, the sweete fresh buds of youth,
The holy dew of prayer lies like pearle,
Dropt from the opening eye-lids of the morne
Upon the bashfull Rose."——

Compare all whitenesse, but himselfe to none,
Glided along, and as he glided watch'd,
And with his *arched neck* this poore fish catch'd."—
Progresse of the Soul, st. 24.

Those highly finished Landscapes, the *Seasons,* are indeed copied from Nature: but *Thomson* sometimes recollected the hand of his Master:

——— ——— " The stately sailing Swan
Gives out his snowy plumage to the gale ;
And arching proud his neck with oary feet,
Bears forward fierce, and guards his osier Isle,
Protective of his young."———

But *to return,* as we say on other occasions— Perhaps the Advocates for *Shakspeare*'s knowledge of the *Latin* language may be more successful. Mr. *Gildon* takes the Van. " It is plain, that he was acquainted with the *Fables* of antiquity very well: that some of the Arrows of *Cupid* are pointed with Lead, and others with Gold, he found in *Ovid;* and what he speaks of *Dido,* in *Virgil:* nor do I know any translation of these Poets so ancient as *Shakspeare*'s time." The passages on which these sagacious remarks are made, occur in the *Midsummer Night's Dream;* and exhibit, we see, a clear proof of acquaintance with the *Latin* Classicks. But we are not answerable for Mr. *Gildon*'s ignorance; he might have been told of *Caxton* and

Douglas, of *Surrey* and *Stanyhurst,* of *Phaer*
and *Twyne,* of *Fleming* and *Golding,* of *Turberville* and *Churchyard!* but these *Fables* were
easily known without the help of either the
originals or the translations. The fate of *Dido*
had been sung very early by *Gower, Chaucer,*
and *Lydgate; Marloe* had even already introduced her to the Stage: and *Cupid*'s arrows appear
with their characteristick differences in *Surrey,*
in *Sidney,* in *Spenser,* and every Sonnetteer of
the time. Nay, their very names were exhibited
long before in the *Romaunt of the Rose;* a work,
you may venture to look into, notwithstanding
Master *Prynne* hath so positively assured us, on
the word of *John Gerson,* that the Author is
most certainly damned, if he did not care for a
serious repentance*.

Mr. *Whalley* argues in the same manner, and
with the same success. He thinks a passage in
the *Tempest,*

————————— " High Queen of State,
Great *Juno* comes; I know her by her *Gait,"*

a remarkable instance of *Shakspeare*'s knowledge of ancient poetick story; and that the

---

* Had our zealous Puritan been acquainted with the
real crime of *De Mehun,* he would not have joined in the
clamour against him. Poor *Jehan,* it seems, had raised the
expectations of a Monastery in *France,* by the Legacy of a

hint was furnished by the *Divûm incedo Regina*
of *Virgil**.

You know, honest *John Taylor*, the *Water-
poet*, declares that *he never learned his Acci-
dence;* and that *Latin and French* were to him
Heathen-Greek; yet by the help of Mr. *Whalley*'s argument, I will prove him a *learned* Man,
in spite of every thing he may say to the contrary; for thus he makes a *Gallant* address his
Lady :—

" Most inestimable Magazine of Beauty—in
whom *the Port and Majesty of Juno*, the Wis-

---

great Chest, and the weighty contents of it; but it proved
to be filled with nothing better than *Vetches*. The Friars,
enraged at the ridicule and disappointment, would not
suffer him to have Christian burial. See the Hon. Mr.
Barrington's very learned and curious *Observations on the
Statutes*, 4to, 1766, p. 24. From the *Annales d'Acquytayne,*
Par. 1537.

Our Author had his full share in distressing the Spirit of
this restless man. " Some Play-books are grown from
Quarto into *Folio ;* which yet bear so good a price and
sale, that I cannot but with griefe relate it.——*Shackspeer*'s
Plaies are printed in the best Crowne-paper, far better than
most *Bibles!*"

* Others would give up this passage for the *Vera incessu
patuit Dea*, but I am not able to see any improvement in
the matter; even supposing the Poet had been speaking of
Juno, and no previous Translation were extant.

dom of *Jove's* braine-bred Girle, and the Feature of *Cytherea**, have their domestical habitation."

In the *Merchant of Venice,* we have an oath " By *two-headed Janus ;*" and here, says Dr. *Warburton, Shakspeare* shews his knowledge in the Antique : and so again does the *Water-poet,* who describes *Fortune*

" Like a *Janus* with a *double-face."*

But *Shakspeare* hath somewhere a *Latin Motto,* quoth Dr. *Sewel ;* and so hath *John Taylor,* and a whole Poem upon it into the bargain.

You perceive, my dear Sir, how vague and in-

---

* This passage recals to my memory a very extraordinary fact. A few years ago, at a great Court on the Continent, a Countryman of our's of high rank and character, [Sir *C. H. W.*] exhibited with many other Candidates his complimental Epigram on the Birth-day, and carried the prize in triumph,

" O Regina orbis prima & pulcherrima : ridens
    Es Venus, incedens Juno, Minerva loquens."
Literally stolen from *Angerianus,*
" Tres quondam nudas vidit Priameius heros
    Luce deas ; video tres quoque luce deas.
Hoc majus ; tres uno in corpore : *Cælia ridens*
    Est Venus, incedens Juno, Minerva loquens."
Delitiæ Ital. Poet. by *Gruter,* under the anagrammatic Name of *Ranutius Gherus,* 1608, V. 1, p. 189.

Perhaps the *latter part* of the Epigram was met with in a whimsical book, which had its day of Fame, *Robert Burton's Anatomy of Melancholy,* Fol. 1652, 6th Edit. p. 520.

G

determinate such arguments must be : for in fact
this *sweet Swan of Thames,* as Mr. *Pope* calls
him, hath more scraps of *Latin* and allusions to
antiquity than are any where to be met with in the
writings of *Shakspeare.* I am sorry to trouble you
with trifles, yet what must be done, when grave
men insist upon them ?

It should seem to be the opinion of some modern criticks, that the personages of classick land
began only to be known in *England* in the time
of *Shakspeare* ; or rather, that he particularly
had the honour of introducing them to the notice
of his countrymen.

For instance,--*Rumour painted full of tongues,*
gives us a Prologue to one of the parts of *Henry
the Fourth;* and, says Dr. *Dodd, Shakspeare*
had doubtless a view to either *Virgil* or *Ovid* in
their description of *Fame.*

But why so ? *Stephen Hawes,* in his *Pastime
of Pleasure,* had long before exhibited her in the
same manner,

> " A goodly Lady envyroned about
> With *tongues* of fyre*."

and so had Sir *Thomas More* in one of his
Pageants† :

> " *Fame* I am called, mervayle you nothing
> Though with *tonges* I am compassed all rounde."

* Cap. 1, 4to, 1555.
† Amongst " the things which Mayster *More* wrote

Not to mention her elaborate Portrait by *Chaucer,*
in the *Boke of Fame;* and by *John Higgins,*
one of the Assistants in the *Mirour for Magis-
trates,* in his Legend of King *Albanacte.*

A very liberal Writer on the *Beauties of
Poetry,* who hath been more conversant in the
ancient Literature of other Countries than his
own, " cannot but wonder, that a Poet, whose
classical Images are composed of the finest parts,
and breathe the very spirit of ancient Mythology,
should pass for being illiterate :"

> " See what a grace was seated on his brow !
> *Hyperion's* curls : the front of *Jove* himself:
> An eye like *Mars* to threaten and command :
> A station like the herald *Mercury,*
> New lighted on a heaven-kissing hill."	*Hamlet.*

Illiterate is an ambiguous term : the question is,
whether Poetick History could be only known by
an Adept in *Languages.* It is no reflection on this
ingenious Gentleman, when I say, that I use on
this occasion the words of a *better* Critick, who
yet was not willing to carry the *illiteracy* of our
Poet *too far :*—" They who are in such astonish-
ment at the *learning* of *Shakspeare,* forget that
the Pagan Imagery was familiar to all the Poets
of his time ; and that abundance of this sort of

in his youth for his pastime," prefixed to his *Workes,*
1557, Fol.

learning was to be picked up from almost every *English* book that he could take into his hands." For not to insist upon *Stephen Bateman*'s Golden Booke of the leaden Goddes, 1577, and several other laborious compilations on the subject, all this and much more Mythology might as perfectly have been learned from the *Testament of Creseide**, and the *Fairy Queen†*, as from a regular *Pantheon*, or *Polymetis* himself.

Mr. *Upton*, not contented with *Heathen* learning, when he finds it in the text, must necessarily superadd it when it appears to be wanting; because *Shakspeare* most certainly hath lost it by accident!

In *Much ado about Nothing*, Don *Pedro* says of the insensible *Benedict*, "He hath twice or thrice cut *Cupid*'s bow-string, and the little *Hangman* dare not shoot at him."

This mythology is not recollected in the Ancients, and therefore the critick hath no doubt but his Author wrote "*Henchman,—a Page, Pusio*: and *this* word seeming too hard for the Printer, he translated the little Urchin into a

---

* Printed amongst the Works of *Chaucer*, but really written by *Robert Henderson*, or *Henryson*, according to other authorities.

† It is observable, that *Hyperion* is used by *Spenser* with the same error in *quantity*.

Hangman, a character no way belonging to him."

But this character was not borrowed from the Ancients ;— it came from the *Arcadia* of Sir *Philip Sidney :*

> " Millions of yeares this old drivell *Cupid* lives ;
> While still more wretch, more wicked he doth prove:
> Till now at length that *Jove* an office gives,
> (At *Juno*'s suite, who much did *Argus* love)
> In this our world a *Hangman* for to be
> Of all those fooles that will have all they see."
>
> B. 2, ch. 14.

I know it may be objected on the authority of such Biographers as *Theophilus Cibber,* and the Writer of the Life of Sir *Philip,* prefixed to the modern Editions, that the *Arcadia* was not published before 1613, and consequently too late for this imitation: but I have a copy in my own possession, printed for *W. Ponsonbie,* 1590, 4to, which hath escaped the notice of the industrious *Ames,* and the rest of our typographical Antiquaries.

Thus likewise every word of antiquity is to be cut down to the classical standard.

In a note on the Prologue to *Troilus and Cressida,* (which, by the way, is not met with in the *Quarto*) Mr. *Theobald* informs us, that the very *names* of the gates of *Troy* have been barbarously

demolished by the Editors: and a deal of learned
dust he makes in setting them right again; much,
however, to Mr. *Heath*'s satisfaction.   Indeed,
the learning is modestly withdrawn from the later
Editions, and we are quietly instructed to read,

> " *Dardan*, and *Thymbria, Ilia, Scæa, Troian,*
> And *Amenorides.*"

But had he looked into the *Troy Boke* of *Lydgate*,
instead of puzzling himself with *Dares Phrygius*,
he would have found the horrid demolition to
have been neither the work of *Shakspeare* nor
his Editors.

> " Therto his cyte | compassed enuyrowne
> Hadde gates VI to entre into the towne:
> The firste of all | and strengest eke with all,
> Largest also | and moste pryncypall,
> Of myghty byldyng | alone pereless,
> Was by the kynge called | *Dardanydes;*
> And in storye | lyke as it is founde,
> *Tymbria* | was named the seconde;
> And the thyrde | called *Helyas,*
> The fourthe gate | hyghte also *Cetheas;*
> The fyfthe *Trojana,* | the syxth *Anthonydes,*
> Stronge and myghty | both in werre and pes*."
>   Lond. empr. by *R. Pynson*, 1513, Fol. b. 2, ch. 11.

* The *Troye Boke* was somewhat modernized, and
reduced into regular Stanzas, about the beginning of the
last century, under the name of the " *Life and Death of
Hector*—who fought a hundred mayne Battailes in open

Our excellent friend Mr. *Hurd* hath borne a noble testimony on our side of the question. " *Shakspeare*," says this true Critick, " owed the felicity of freedom from the bondage of classical

field against the *Grecians;* wherein there were slaine on both sides *Fourteene Hundred and Sixe Thousand Four-score and Sixe men.*" *Fol. no date.* This work, Dr. *Fuller* and several other criticks have erroneously quoted as the *Original;* and observe in consequence, that " if *Chaucer's Coin* were of *greater weight* for *deeper learning, Lydgate's* were of a more *refined standard* for *purer language:* so that one might mistake him for a modern Writer !"

Let me here make an observation for the benefit of the next Editor of *Chaucer.* Mr. *Urry,* probably misled by his predecessor, *Speght,* was determined, *Procrustes-like,* to *force* every line in the *Canterbury Tales* to the same Standard : but a precise number of Syllables was not the Object of our old Poets. *Lydgate,* after the example of his Master, very fairly acknowledges,

" Well wot I | moche thing is wronge,
Falsely metryd | both of short and longe."

and *Chaucer* himself was persuaded, that the *Rime* might possibly be

———————— " Somewhat agreáble,
Though some Verse faile in a Sylláble."

In short, the attention was directed to the *Cæsural pause,* as the *Grammarians* call it; which is carefully *marked* in every line of *Lydgate :* and *Gascoigne,* in his *Certayne Notes of Instruction concerning the making of Verse,* observes very truly of *Chaucer,* " Whosoeuer do peruse and well consider his workes, he shall find, that although his lines

superstition to the *want* of what is called the *advantage* of a learned Education. This, as well as a vast superiority of Genius, hath contributed to lift this astonishing man to the glory of being esteemed the most original *thinker* and *speaker* since the times of *Homer.*" And hence indisputably the amazing variety of style and manner, unknown to all other Writers; an argument of *itself* sufficient to emancipate *Shakspeare* from the supposition of a *Classical training.* Yet, to be honest, *one* Imitation is *fastened* on our Poet, which hath been insisted upon likewise by Mr. *Upton* and Mr. *Whalley.* You remember it in the famous Speech of *Claudio* in *Measure for Measure :*

" Ay, but to die, and go we know not where !" &c.

Most certainly the Ideas of a "Spirit bathing in fiery floods," of residing " in thrilling regions of thick-ribbed ice," or of being " imprisoned in

are not alwayes of one selfe same number of Syllables, yet beyng redde by one that hath understanding, the longest verse, and that which hath most syllables in it, will fall to the Eare correspondent unto that which hath fewest syllables in it : and likewise that whiche hath in it fewest syllables shall be founde yet to consist of wordes that hath suche naturall sounde, as may seeme equall in length to a verse which hath many moe syllables of lighter accents." 4to, 1575.

the viewless winds," are not *original* in our Author ; but I am not sure, that they came from the *Platonick Hell* of *Virgil**. The Monks also had their hot and their cold Hell; " The fyrste is fyre that ever brenneth, and never gyveth lighte," says an old Homily✝ :—" The seconde is passyng colde, that yf a grete hylle of fyre were casten therin, it sholde torne to yce." One of their Legends, well remembered in the time of *Shakspeare,* gives us a Dialogue between a Bishop and a Soul tormented in a piece of ice, which was brought to cure *a grete brenning heate* in his foot✝ : take care you do not interpret this the *Gout,* for I remember M. *Menage* quotes a *Canon* upon us,

" Si quis dixerit Episcopum PODAGRA laborare, Anathema sit."

Another tells us of the Soul of a Monk fastened to a Rock, which the winds were to blow about for a twelvemonth, and purge of its enormities.

* ———. ——— " Aliæ panduntur inanes
Suspensæ ad ventos : aliis sub gurgite vasto
Infectum eluitur scelus, aut exuritur igni."

✝ At the ende of the *Festyuall,* drawen oute of *Legenda Aurea,* 4to, 1508 : it was first printed by *Caxton,* 1483, " in helpe of such Clerkes who excuse theym for defaute of bokes, and also by symplenes of connynge."

✝ *On All Soules Daye,* p. 152.

H

Indeed this doctrine was before now introduced into poetick fiction, as you may see in a Poem " where the Lover declareth his pains to exceed far the pains of Hell," among the many miscellaneous ones subjoined to the Works of *Surrey*. Nay, a very learned and inquisitive Brother-Antiquary, our *Greek* Professor, hath observed 'to me on the authority of *Blefkenius,* that this was the ancient opinion of the inhabitants of *Iceland**, who were certainly very little read either in the *Poet* or the *Philosopher.*

After all, *Shakspeare*'s curiosity might lead him to *Translations.*   *Gawin Douglas* really changes the *Platonick Hell* into the " punytion of Saulis in Purgatory:" and it is observable, that when the *Ghost* informs *Hamlet* of his Doom there,

> " Till the foul crimes done in his days of nature
> Are *burnt and purg'd away*,"——

the Expression is very similar to the Bishop's : I will give you his Version as concisely as I can ; " It is a nedeful thyng to suffer panis and torment —Sum in the wyndis, sum under the watter, and in the fire uthir sum:—thus the mony Vices—

> " Contrakkit in the corpis be *done away*
> And *purgit.*"——
> > *Sixte Booke of Eneados,* Fol. p. 191.

* *Islandiæ* Descript. *Ludg. Bat.* 1607, p. 46.

It seems, however, " that *Shakspeare himself*
in the *Tempest* hath translated some expressions
of *Virgil:* witness the *O Dea certe.*" I pre-
sume, we are here directed to the passage, where
Ferdinand says of *Miranda*, after hearing the
Songs of *Ariel*,

—————————— " Most sure, the Goddess
On whom these airs attend ;"

and so *very small Latin* is sufficient for this formidable translation, that, if it be thought any
honour to our Poet, I am loth to deprive him of
it ; but his honour is not built on such a sandy
foundation.   Let us turn to a *real Translator*,
and examine whether the Idea might not be fully
comprehended by an *English* reader, *supposing* it
necessarily borrowed from *Virgil*.   *Hexameters*
in our own language are almost forgotten ; we
will quote therefore this time from *Stanyhurst :*

" O to thee, fayre Virgin, what terme may rightly be
    fitted ?
Thy tongue, thy visage no mortal frayltie resembleth.
—— *No doubt, a Godesse !*"   Edit. 1583.

Gabriel Harvey desired only to be " *Epitaph'd*,
the Inventor of the *English Hexameter*," and
for a while every one would be *halting on Roman
feet ;* but the ridicule of our Fellow-Collegian
Hall, in one of his *Satires*, and the reasoning of

Daniel, in his *Defence of Rhyme* against *Campion,* presently reduced us to our original *Gothic.*

But to come nearer the purpose, what will you say, if I can shew you that *Shakspeare,* when, in the favourite phrase, he had a *Latin* Poet *in his Eye,* most assuredly made use of a Translation ?

Prospero, in the *Tempest,* begins the Address to his attendant *Spirits,*

" Ye Elves of Hills, of standing Lakes and Groves."

This speech, Dr. *Warburton* rightly observes to be borrowed from *Medea* in *Ovid;* and " it proves, says Mr. *Holt*,* beyond contradiction, that *Shakspeare* was perfectly acquainted with the Sentiments of the Ancients on the Subject of Inchantments." The original lines are these :

" Auræque, & venti, montesque, amnesque, lacusque,
Diique omnes nemorum, diique omnes noctis adeste."

It happens, however, that the translation by *Arthur Golding*† is by no means literal, and *Shakspeare* hath closely followed it :

---

* In some Remarks on the *Tempest,* published under the quaint Title of " An Attempte to rescue that aunciente English Poet and Play-wrighte, Maister *Williaume Shakespeare,* from the many Errours, faulsely charged upon him by certaine new-fangled Wittes." *Lond.* 8vo, 1749, p. 81.

† His work is dedicated to the Earl of *Leicester* in a long Epistle in verse, from *Berwicke,* April 20, 1567.

" Ye Ayres and Winds ; *Ye Elves of Hills,* of Brookes,
of Woods alone,
" *Of standing Lakes,* and of the Night, approche ye
everych one."

I think it is unnecessary to pursue this any
further, especially as more powerful arguments
await us.

In the *Merchant of Venice,* the *Jew,* as an
apology for his cruelty to *Anthonio,* rehearses
many *Sympathies* and *Antipathies* for which *no
reason can be rendered :*

" Some love not a gaping Pig——
And others, when the *Bagpipe* sings i' th' nose,
Cannot contain their urine for *affection.*"

This incident, Dr. *Warburton* supposes to be
taken from a passage in *Scaliger's Exercitations*
against *Cardan,* " Narrabo tibi jocosam Sympa-
thiam *Reguli, Vasconis* Equitis : Is dum viveret
audito *Phormingis* sono, urinam illico facere
cogebatur." And, proceeds the *Doctor,* to make
this jocular story still more ridiculous, *Shakspeare,* I suppose, translated *Phorminx* by *Bag-
pipes.*

Here we seem fairly caught ;—for *Scaliger's*
work was never, as the term goes, *done into
English.* But luckily in an old translation from
the *French* of *Peter le Loier,* entitled, *A Treatise
of Specters, or straunge Sights, Visions and*

Apparitions appearing sensibly unto Men, we have this identical Story from *Scaliger;* and what is still more, a marginal Note gives us, in all probability, the very fact alluded to, as well as the word of *Shakspeare :* " Another Gentleman of this quality liued of late in Deuon neere Excester, who could not endure the playing on a *Bagpipe*.*"

We may just add, as some observation hath been made upon it, that *Affection* in the sense of *Sympathy* was formerly *technical;* and so used by Lord *Bacon,* Sir *Kenelm Digby,* and many other Writers.

A single word in Queen *Catherine*'s Character of *Wolsey,* in *Henry* VIII, is brought by the *Doctor* as another argument for the learning of *Shakspeare.*

—————————— " He was a man
Of an unbounded Stomach, ever ranking
Himself with Princes; one that by *Suggestion*
Ty'd all the kingdom. Simony was fair play.
His own opinion was his law, i' th' presence
He would say untruths, and be ever double
Both in his words and meaning. He was never,
But where he meant to ruin, pitiful.
His promises were, as he then was, mighty;
But his performance, as he now is, nothing.
Of his own body he was ill, and gave
The Clergy ill example."

* M. *Bayle* hath delineated the singular character of our

The word *Suggestion*, says the Critick, is here used with great propriety, and *seeming* knowledge of the Latin tongue: and he proceeds to settle the sense of it from *the late Roman writers and their glossers.* But *Shakspeare*'s knowledge was from *Holingshed*, whom he follows *verbatim:*

" This Cardinal was of a great stomach, for he compted himself equal with princes, and by craftie *Suggestion* got into his hands innumerable treasure: he forced little on simonie, and was not pitifull, and stood affectionate in his own opinion: in open presence he would lie and seie untruth, and was double both in speech and meaning: he would promise much and performe little: he was vicious of his bodie, and gaue the clergie euil example." Edit. 1587, p. 922.

Perhaps, after this quotation, you may not think that Sir *Thomas Hanmer*, who reads *Tyth'd*—instead of *Ty'd all the kingdom,* deserves quite so much of Dr. *Warburton*'s severity. Indisputably the passage, like every other in the Speech, is intended to express the meaning of the parallel

fantastical Author. His work was originally translated by one *Zacharie Jones.* My Edit. is in 4to, 1605, with an anonymous Dedication to the King: the *Devonshire* Story was therefore well known in the time of *Shakspeare.*—— The passage from *Scaliger* is likewise to be met with in *The Optick Glasse of Humors*, written, I believe, by *T. Wombwell;* and in several other places.

one in the Chronicle: it cannot therefore be cre-
dited, that any man, when the *Original* was produced, should still chuse to defend a *cant* accep-
tation; and inform us, perhaps, *seriously*, that in
gaming language, from I know not what practice, to *tye* is to *equal!* A sense of the word, as
far as I have yet found, *unknown* to our old
Writers; and, if *known*, would not surely have
been used in *this* place by our Author.

But let us turn from conjecture to *Shakspeare's*
authorities. *Hall*, from whom the above description is copied by *Holingshed*, is very explicit in
the demands of the *Cardinal:* who having inso-
lently told the *Lord Mayor* and *Aldermen*, " For
sothe I thinke, that *halfe* your substaunce were to
litle," assures them, by way of comfort at the end
of his harangue, that *upon an average* the *tythe*
should be sufficient; " Sers, speake not to breake
that thyng that is concluded, for *some* shal not
paie the *tenth* parte, and *some* more."—And again;
" Thei saied, the Cardinall by Visitacions, makyng
of Abbottes, probates of testamentes, graunting
of faculties, licences, and other pollyngs in his
Courtes legantines, had made his *threasore egall
with the kynges*." Edit. 1548, p. 138, and 143.

Skelton*, in his *Why come ye not to Court,*

* His Poems are printed with the title of " Pithy, Pleasaunt, and Profitable Workes of Maister *Skelton, Poete*

gives us, after his rambling manner, a curious character of *Wolsey* :—

Laureate."—But, says Mr. *Cibber*, after several other Writers, " how or by what Interest he was made *Laureat,* or whether it was a title he assumed to himself, cannot be determined."——This is an error pretty generally received, and it may be worth our while to remove it.

A facetious Author says somewhere, that a *Poet Laureat,* in the modern Idea, is a Gentleman, who hath an annual Stipend for reminding us of the *New Year,* and the *Birthday ;* but formerly a *Poet Laureat* was a real *University Graduate.*

> " *Skelton* wore the Lawrell wreath,
> And past in *schoels* ye knoe,"

says *Churchyarde* in the Poem prefixed to his Works. And Master *Caxton* in his Preface to *The Boke of Eneydos,* 1490, hath a passage, which well deserves to be quoted without abridgment : " I praye mayster *John Skelton, late created poete laureate in the unyversite of Oxenforde,* to oversee and correcte thys sayd booke, and taddresse and expowne whereas shall be founde faulte, to theym that shall requyre it : for hym I knowe for suffycyent to expowne and Englysshe every dyfficulte that is therein ; for he hath late translated the epystles of *Tulle,* and the book of *Dyodorus Syculus,* and diverse other workes, out of *Latyn* into *Englisshe,* not in rude and old language, but in polyshed and ornate termes, craftely, as he that hath redde *Vyrgyle, Ouyde, Tullye,* and all the other noble poets and oratours, to me unknowen : and also he hath redde the ix muses, and understands their musicalle scyences, and to whom of them eche scyence is appropred : I suppose he hath dronken of *Elycons* well !"

I find, from Mr. *Baker's* MSS. that our *Laureat* was

I

————— " By and by

He will drynke us so dry

And sucke us so nye

That men shall scantly

Haue penny or halpennye

God saue hys noble grace

And graunt him a place

Endlesse to dwel

With the deuill of hel

For and he were there

We nead neuer feare

Of the feendes blacke

For I   undertake

He wold so brag and crake

That he wold than make

The deuils to quake

To shudder and to shake

Lyke a fier drake

And with a cole rake

Bruse them on a brake

And binde them to a stake

And set hel on fyre

At his owne desire

He is such a grym syre !"   Edit. 1568.

admitted *ad eundem* at *Cambridge:* " An. Dom. 1493. &
Hen. 7. nono. Conceditur *Johi Skelton* Poete in partibus
transmarinis atque *Oxon.* Laureâ ornato, ut apud nos
eâdem decoraretur." And afterward, " An. 150⅘ Conceditur *Johi Skelton,* Poetæ Laureat. quod possit stare eodem
gradu hic, quo stetit *Oxoniis,* & quod possit uti habitu
sibi concesso à Principe."

See likewise Dr. *Knight's* Life of *Colet,* p. 122. And
Recherches sur les *Poetes couronnez,* par M. l'Abbé *du
Resnel,* in the *Memoires de Litterature,* vol. 10, *Paris,*
4to, 1736.

Mr. *Upton* and some other Criticks have thought it very *scholar-like* in *Hamlet* to swear the Centinels on a *Sword;* but this is for ever met with.   For instance, in the *Passus primus* of *Pierce Plowman,*

" *David* in his daies dubbed knightes,
And did hem *swere on her sword* to serue truth euer."

And in *Hieronymo,* the common Butt of our Author, and the Wits of the time, says *Lorenzo* to *Pendringano,*

" Swear on this cross, that what thou sayst is true—
But if I prove thee perjured and unjust,
This very *sword,* whereon thou took'st thine oath,
Shall be the worker of thy Tragedy !"

We have therefore no occasion to go with **Mr.** *Garrick* as far as the *French* of *Brantôme* to illustrate this ceremony *; a *Gentleman,* who will be always allowed the *first Commentator* on *Shakspeare,* when he does not carry us beyond *himself.*

Mr. *Upton* however, in the next place, produces a passage from *Henry the Sixth,* whence he argues it to be very plain that our Author had not only *read Cicero's Offices,* but even more *critically* than many of the Editors :

* Mr. *Johnson's* Edit. v. 8, p. 171.

———————— " This Villain here,
Being Captain of a *Pinnace,* threatens more
Than *Bargulus,* the strong *Illyrian* Pirate."

So the *Wight,* he observes with great exultation,
is named by *Cicero* in the Editions of *Shakspeare*'s time, " *Bargulus Illyrius* latro ;" tho'
the modern Editors have chosen to call him
Bardylis :—" and *thus* I found it in *two* MSS."
———And *thus* he might have found it in *two*
Translations, before *Shakspeare* was born.—
Robert Whytinton, 1533, calls him, " *Bargulus*
a Pirate upon the see of *Illiry ;*" and *Nicholas
Grimald,* about twenty years afterward, " *Bargulus* the *Illyrian* Robber *."

But it had been easy to have checked Mr.
Upton's exultation, by observing that *Bargulus*
does not appear in the *Quarto ;* which also is
the case with some fragments of *Latin* verses, in
the different *parts* of this *doubtful* performance.

It is scarcely worth mentioning, that two or
three more *Latin* passages, which are met with
in our Author, are immediately transcribed from
the Story or Chronicle before him. Thus in

———————

* I have met with a Writer who tells us, that a Translation of the *Offices* was printed by *Caxton* in the year
1481 : but such a book never existed. It is a mistake for
" *Tullius of olde age,*" printed with the *Boke of Frendshipe,*
by *John Tiptoft,* Earl of *Worcester.* I believe the former
was translated by *Wyllyam Wyrcestre,* alias *Botoner.*

Henry the Fifth, whose right to the kingdom of *France* is copiously demonstrated by the *Archbishop* :—

——————— " There is no bar
To make against your Highness' claim to *France,*
But this which they produce from *Pharamond:*
In terram *Salicam* mulieres nè succedant;
No Woman shall succeed in *Salike* land:
Which *Salike* land the *French* unjustly gloze
To be the realm of *France,* and *Pharamond*
The founder of this law and female bar.
Yet their own authors faithfully affirm,
That the land *Salike* lies in *Germany,*
Between the floods of *Sala* and of *Elve,*" &c.

Archbishop *Chichelie,* says *Holingshed,* " did much inueie against the surmised and false fained law *Salike,* which the *Frenchmen* alledge euer against the kings of *England* in barre of their just title to the crowne of *France.* The very words of that supposed law are these, In terram *Salicam* mulieres nè succedant, that is to saie, Into the *Salike* land let not women succeed; which the *French* glossers expound to be the realm of *France,* and that this law was made by King *Pharamond:* whereas yet their owne authors affirme, that the land *Salike* is in *Germanie,* between the rivers of *Elbe* and *Sala,*" &c. p. 545.

It hath lately been repeated from Mr. *Guthrie*'s " Essay upon *English* Tragedy," that the

Portrait of *Macbeth's Wife* is copied from *Buchanan,* "whose spirit, as well as words, is translated into the Play of *Shakspeare :* and it had signified nothing to have pored only on *Holingshed* for *Facts."*——"Animus etiam, per se ferox, prope quotidianis conviciis uxoris (quæ omnium consiliorum ei erat conscia) stimulabatur."—This is the whole that *Buchanan* says of the *Lady,* and truly I see no more *spirit* in the *Scotch,* than in the *English* Chronicler. " The wordes of the three weird Sisters also greatly encouraged him [to the Murder of *Duncan*], but specially his wife lay sore upon him to attempt the thing, as she that was very ambitious, brenning in unquenchable desire to beare the name of a Queene." Edit. 1577, p. 244.

This part of *Holingshed* is an Abridgment of *Johne Bellenden's* translation of the *noble clerk, Hector Boece, imprinted* at *Edingburgh,* in *Fol.* 1541. I will give the passage as it is found there. " His wyfe impacient of lang tary (*as all wemen ar*) specially quhare they ar desirus of ony purpos, gaif hym gret artation to pursew the thrid weird, that sche micht be ane quene, calland hym oft tymis febyl cowart and nocht desyrus of honouris, sen he durst not assailze the thing with manheid and curage, quhilk is offerit to hym be beniuolence of fortoun. Howbeit sindry otheris hes assailzeit sic thinges afore with maist terribyl jeopardyis, quhen they had not sic sickernes to succeid in the end of thair lauboris as he had." P. 173.

But we can *demonstrate* that *Shakspeare* had not the Story from *Buchanan*. According to *him*, the Weïrd-Sisters salute *Macbeth*, "Una *Angusiœ* Thanum, altera *Moraviœ*, tertia *Regem*." Thane of *Angus*, and of *Murray*, &c.; but according to *Holingshed*, immediately from *Bellenden*, as it stands in *Shakspeare*, "The first of them spake and sayde, All hayle *Makbeth*, Thane of *Glammis*,—the second of them said, Hayle *Makbeth*, Thane of *Cawder;* but the third sayde, All hayle *Makbeth*, that hereafter shall be *king of Scotland*." P. 243.

> " 1 *Witch*. All hail, *Macbeth !* Hail to thee, *Thane* of *Glamis !*
>
> 2 *Witch*. All hail, *Macbeth !* Hail to thee, Thane of *Cawdor !*
>
> 3 *Witch*. All hail, *Macbeth!* that shall be *King* hereafter !"

Here too our Poet found the equivocal Predictions, on which his Hero so fatally depended. " He had learned of certain wysards, how that he ought to take heede of *Macduffe ;*——and surely hereupon had he put *Macduffe* to death, but a certaine witch, whom he had in great trust, had tolde, that he should neuer be slain with *man borne of any woman*, nor vanquished till the

Wood of *Bernane* came to the Castell of *Dunsinane.*" p. 244. And the Scene between *Malcolm* and *Macduff* in the fourth act is almost literally taken from the *Chronicle.*

Macbeth was certainly one of *Shakspeare*'s latest Productions, and it might possibly have been suggested to him by a little performance on the same subject at *Oxford* before King *James,* 1605. I will transcribe my notice of it from *Wake's Rex Platonicus :* "Fabulæ ansam dedit antiqua de Regiâ prosapiâ historiola apud *Scoto-Britannos* celebrata, quæ narrat tres olim Sibyllas occurrisse duobus *Scotiæ* proceribus, *Macbetho* & *Banchoni,* & illum prædixisse Regem futurum, sed Regem nullum geniturum ; hunc Regem non futurum, sed Reges geniturum multos. Vaticinii veritatem rerum eventus comprobavit. *Banchonis* enim è stirpe Potentissimus *Jacobus* oriundus." p. 29.

A stronger argument hath been brought from the Plot of *Hamlet.* Dr. *Grey* and Mr. *Whalley* assure us, that for *this, Shakspeare must* have read *Saxo Grammaticus* in *Latin,* for no translation hath been made into any modern language. But the truth is, he did not take it from *Saxo* at all ; a Novel called the *Hystorie of Hamblet* was his original : a fragment of which, in *black letter,* I have been favoured with by a very curious and intelligent Gentleman, to whom the lovers of *Shakspeare* will some time or other owe great obligations.

It hath indeed been said, that, " IF *such an history exists,* it is almost impossible that any poet unacquainted with the *Latin* language (supposing his perceptive faculties to have been ever so acute) could have caught the characteristical madness of *Hamlet,* described by *Saxo Grammaticus**, so happily as it is delineated by *Shakspeare.*

Very luckily, our Fragment gives us a part of *Hamlet's* Speech to his *Mother,* which sufficiently replies to this observation.—" It was not without cause, and juste occasion, that my gestures, countenances and words seeme to proceed from a madman, and that I desire to haue all men esteeme mee wholy depriued of sence and reasonable understanding, bycause I am well assured that he that hath made no conscience to kill his owne brother, (accustomed to murthers, and allured with desire of gouernement without controll in his treasons) will not spare to saue himselfe with the like crueltie, in the blood and flesh of the

---

* " Falsitatis enim *(Hamlethus)* alienus haberi cupidus, ita astutiam veriloquio permiscebat, ut nec dictis veracitas deesset, nec acuminis modus verorum judicio proderetur." This is quoted, as it had been before, in Mr. *Guthrie's* Essay on Tragedy, with a *small* variation from the *Original.* See Edit. *Fol.* 1644, p. 50.

K

loyns of his brother, by him massacred: and
therefore it is better for me to fayne madnesse
then to use my right sences as nature hath
bestowed them upon me. The bright shining
clearnes therof I am forced to hide vnder this
shadow of dissimulation, as the sun doth hir
beams vnder some great cloud, when the wether
in summer time ouercasteth: the face of a mad
man serueth to couer my gallant countenance,
and the gestures of a fool are fit for me, to the
end that guiding my self wisely therin I may pre-
serue my life for the *Danes* and the memory of
my late deceased father, for that the desire of
reuenging his death is so ingrauen in my heart,
that if I dye not shortly, I hope to take such and
so great vengeance, that these Countryes shall
for euer speake thereof. Neuerthelesse I must
stay the time, meanes, and occasion, lest by
making ouer great hast, I be now the cause of
mine owne sodaine ruine and ouerthrow, and by
that meanes, end, before I beginne to effect my
hearts desire: hee that hath to doe with a
wicked, disloyall, cruell, and discourteous man,
must vse craft, and politike inuentions, such as a
fine witte can best imagine, not to discouer his
interprise: for seeing that by force I cannot
effect my desire, reason alloweth me by dissimu_
lation, subtiltie, and secret practises, to proceed
therein."

But to put the matter out of all question, my communicative Friend above-mentioned, Mr. *Capell*, (for why should I not give myself the credit of his name?) hath been fortunate enough to procure from the Collection of the Duke of *Newcastle*, a *complete* Copy of the *Hystorie of Hamblet*, which proves to be a translation from the *French* of *Belleforest*; and he tells me, that " all the chief incidents of the Play, and all the capital Characters are there in *embryo*, after a rude and barbarous manner : sentiments indeed there are none that *Shakspeare* could borrow ; nor any expression but *one*, which is, where *Hamlet* kills *Polonius* behind the arras ; in doing which he is made to cry out, as in the Play, " *a rat, a rat !*"——So much for *Saxo Grammaticus !*

It is scarcely conceivable, how industriously the puritanical Zeal of the last age exerted itself in destroying, amongst better things, the innocent amusements of the former. Numberless *Tales* and *Poems* are alluded to in old Books, which are now perhaps no where to be found. Mr. *Capell* informs me, (and he is, in these matters, the most able of all men to give information) that our Author appears to have been beholden to some *Novels*, which he hath yet only seen in *French* or *Italian :* but he adds, "to say they are not in some *English* dress, prosaic or metrical, and perhaps with circumstances nearer to his stories, is what I will not take upon me to do: nor indeed is it what I believe; but rather the contrary, and that time and accident will bring some of them to light, if not all."——

W. Painter, at the conclusion of the second *Tome* of his *Palace of Pleasure,* 1567, *advertises* the Reader, "bicause sodaynly (contrary to expectation) this Volume is risen to greater heape of leaues, I doe omit for this present time *sundry Nouels* of mery deuise, reseruing the same to be joyned with the rest of an other part, wherein shall succeede the remnant of *Bandello,* specially sutch (suffrable) as the learned French man *François de Belleforrest* hath selected, and the choysest done in the *Italian.* Some also out of *Erizzo, Ser Giouanni Florentino, Parabosco, Cynthio, Straparole, Sansouino,* and the best liked out of the Queene of *Nauarre,* and other Authors. Take these in good part, with those that haue and shall come forth."——But I am not able to find, that a *third Tome* was ever published; and it is very probable, that the Interest of his Booksellers, and more especially the prevailing Mode of the time, might lead him afterward to print his *sundry Novels* separately. If this were the case, it is no wonder that such *fugitive Pieces* ere recovered with difficulty; when the *two Tomes,* which *Tom. Rawlinson* would have called *justa Volumina,* are almost annihilated. Mr. *Ames,* who searched after books of this sort with the utmost avidity, most certainly had not seen them, when he published his *Typographical Antiquities,* as appears from his blunders about them: and possibly I myself might have remained in the same predicament, had I not been favoured with a Copy by my generous Friend, Mr. *Lort.*

Mr. *Colman,* in the Preface to his elegant Translation of *Terence,* hath offered some arguments for the Learning of *Shakspeare,* which have been retailed with much confidence since the appearance of Mr. *Johnson's* Edition.

"Besides the resemblance of particular passages scattered up and down in different plays, it is well known, that the *Comedy of Errours* is in great measure founded on the *Menœchmi* of *Plautus;* but I do not recollect ever to have seen it observed, that the disguise of the *Pedant* in the *Taming of the Shrew,* and his assuming the name and character of *Vincentio,* seem to be evidently taken from the disguise of the *Syco-phanta* in the *Trinummus* of the said Author* ;

* This observation of Mr. *Colman* is quoted by his very ingenious Colleague, Mr. *Thornton,* in his Translation of this Play; who further remarks, in another part of it, that a passage in *Romeo and Juliet,* where *Shakspeare* speaks of the *contradiction* in the nature of *Love,* is very much in the manner of his Author:

and there is a quotation from the *Eunuch* of
Terence also, so familiarly introduced into the

" Amor—mores hominum moros & morosos efficit.
Minus placet quod suadetur, quod disuadetur placet.
Quom inopia'st, cupias, quando ejus copia'st tum non
    velis." &c.

Which he translates with ease and elegance,
———————— " Love makes a man a fool,
Hard to be pleas'd.——What you'd persuade him to,
He likes not, and embraces that, from which
You would dissuade him.—What there is a lack of,
That will he covet ;—when 'tis in his power,
He'll none on't."——   *Act* 3, *Scene* 3.

Let us now turn to the passage in *Shakspeare :*
——— " O brawling Love ! O loving hate ! ———
O heavy lightness ! serious vanity !
Mis-shapen Chaos of well-seeming forms !
Feather of lead, bright smoke, cold fire, sick health !
Still-waking Sleep ! that is not what it is !"

Shakspeare, I am sure, in the opinion of Mr. *Thornton*,
did not want a *Plautus* to teach him the workings of Nature ; nor are his *Parallelisms* produced with any such im-
plication : but, I suppose, a peculiarity appears here in
the manner of expression, which however was extremely
the humour of the Age. Every *Sonnetteer* characterises
Love by contrarieties. *Watson* begins one of his *Canzonets*,

    " Love is a sowre delight, a sugred griefe,
      A living death, an euer-dying life," &c.

Turberville makes *Reason* harangue against it in the same
manner :

    " A fierie Frost, a Flame that frozen is with Ise !
    A heavie Burden light to bear ! a Vertue fraught with
      Vice !" &c.

Dialogue of the *Taming of the Shrew*, that I think it puts the question of *Shakspeare*'s having read the Roman Comick Poets in the *original* language out of all doubt :—

" Redime te captum, quam queas, minimo."

With respect to *resemblances*, I shall not trouble you any further.—That the *Comedy of Errors* is founded on the *Menœchmi*, it is notorious : nor is it less so, that a Translation of it by

Immediately from the *Romaunt of the Rose*,

" Loue it is an hatefull pees
A free acquitaunce without reles—
An heavie burthen light to beare,
A wicked wawe awaie to weare ;
And health full of maladie,
And charitie full of envie—
A laughter that is weping aie
Rest that trauaileth night and daie," &c.

This kind of *Antithesis* was very much the taste of the *Provençal* and *Italian* Poets ; perhaps it might be hinted by the Ode of *Sappho* preserved by *Longinus: Petrarch* is full of it,

" Pace non trovo, & non hó do far guerra,
Et temo, & spero, & ardo, & son un ghiaccio,
Et volo sopra'l cielo, & ghiaccio in terra,
Et nulla stringo, & tutto'l mondo abbraccio." &c.

Sonetto 105.

Sir *Thomas Wyat* gives a translation of this Sonnet, without any notice of the *Original,* under the title of " Description of the contrarious Passions in a Louer." Amongst the *Songes and Sonettes,* by the Earle of *Surrey,* and Others, 1574.

W. W. perhaps *William Warner*, the Author of *Albion's England*, was extant in the time of *Shakspeare**; though Mr. *Upton* and some other advocates for his learning have cautiously dropt the mention of it. Besides this, (if indeed it were different) in the *Gesta Grayorum*, the Christmas Revels of the *Gray's-Inn* Gentlemen, 1594, " a *Comedy of Errors* like to *Plautus* his *Menœchmus* was played by the Players." And the same hath been suspected to be the subject of the *goodlie Comedie of Plautus* acted at *Greenwich* before the King and Queen in 1520, as we learn from *Hall* and *Holingshed* :—*Riccoboni* highly compliments the *English* on opening their stage so well; but unfortunately, *Cavendish*, in his Life of *Wolsey*, calls it, an *excellent Interlude in Latine.* About the same time it was exhibited in *German* at *Nuremburgh*, by the celebrated *Hanssach* the *Shoemaker.*

" But a character in the *Taming of the Shrew* is borrowed from the *Trinummus*, and no translation of *that* was extant."

---

* It was published in 4to, 1595. The Printer of *Langbaine*, p. 524, hath accidentally given the date, 1515, which hath been copied implicitly by *Gildon, Theobald, Cooke, and several others. Warner* is now almost forgotten, yet the old Criticks esteemed him one of " our chiefe heroical *Makers*."—*Meres* informs us, that he had " heard him termed of the best wits of both our Universities, our *English Homer*."

Mr. *Colman* indeed hath been better employed; but if he had met with an old Comedy, called *Supposes,* translated from *Ariosto* by *George Gascoigne**, he certainly would not have appealed to *Plautus.* Thence *Shakspeare* borrowed this part of the Plot, (as well as some of the phrase-ology) though *Theobald* pronounces it his own invention: there likewise he found the quaint name of *Petruchio.* My young Master and his Man exchange habits and characters, and persuade a *Scenæse,* as he is called, to personate the *Father,* exactly as in the *Taming of the Shrew,* by the pretended danger of his coming from *Sienna* to *Ferrara,* contrary to the order of the government.

Still *Shakspeare* quotes a line from the *Eunuch* of *Terence ;* by memory too, and what is more, " purposely alters it, in order to bring the sense within the compass of one line."——This remark was previous to Mr. *Johnson*'s, or indisputably

* His works were first collected under the singular title of " A hundreth sundrie Flowres bounde up in one small Poesie. Gathered partly (by translation) in the fyne out-landish Gardins of *Euripides, Ouid, Petrarke, Ariosto,* and others ; and partly by inuention, out of our owne fruitefull Orchardes in *Englande :* yelding sundrie sweete sauours of Tragical, Comical, and Morall Discourses, bothe pleasaunt and profitable to the well smellyng noses of learned Readers." *Black Letter,* 4to, no date.

it would not have been made at all.——"Our
Authour had this line from *Lilly ;* which I mention that it may not be brought as an argument
of his learning."

But how, cries an unprovoked Antagonist, can
you take upon you to say, that he had it from
Lilly, and not from *Terence*?* I will answer for
Mr. *Johnson,* who is above answering for him-
self,—Because it is quoted as it appears in the
Grammarian, and not as it appears in the *Poet.*
And thus we have done with the *purposed* alteration.
Udall likewise in his " *Floures for Latin speaking,*
gathered oute of *Terence,* 1560," reduces the pas-
sage to a single line, and subjoins a Translation.

We have hitherto supposed *Shakspeare* the
Author of the *Taming of the Shrew,* but his
property in it is extremely disputable. I will
give you my opinion, and the reasons on which
it is founded. I suppose then the present Play
nor *originally* the work of *Shakspeare,* but re-
stored by him to the Stage, with the whole
Induction of the *Tinker,* and some other occasional improvements ; especially in the Character
of *Petruchio.* It is very obvious, that the
Induction and the *Play* were either the works of
different hands, or written at a great interval of

---

* *W. Kenrick's* Review of Dr. *Johnson's* Edit. of *Shakspeare,* 1765, 8vo, p. 105.

time : the former is in our Author's *best* manner, and the greater part of the *latter* in his *worst,* or even below it. Dr. *Warburton* declares it to be *certainly* spurious : and without doubt, *supposing* it to have been written by *Shakspeare,* it must have been one of his *earliest* productions ; yet it is not mentioned in the List of his Works by *Meres* in 1598.

I have met with a facetious piece of Sir *John Harrington,* printed in 1596, (and possibly there may be an earlier Edition) called, *The Metamorphosis of Ajax,* where I suspect an allusion to the old Play : " Read the *booke* of *Taming a Shrew,* which hath made a number of us so perfect, that *now* every one can rule a Shrew in our Countrey, save he that hath hir."—I am aware, a *modern* Linguist may object, that the word *Book* does not at present seem *dramatick,* but it was once almost *technically* so : *Gosson* in his Schoole of Abuse, contayning a pleasaunt inuective against *Poets, Pipers, Players, Jesters,* and such like *Caterpillars* of a Common-wealth, 1579, mentions " twoo prose *Bookes* plaied at the *Belsauage ;*" and *Hearne* tells us in a Note at the end of *William of Worcester,* that he had seen " a MS. in the nature of a *Play* or *Interlude,* intitled, the *Booke* of Sir *Thomas Moore*.*"

* I know, indeed, there is extant a very old Poem, in

And, in fact, there is such an old *anonymous*
Play in Mr. *Pope*'s List. " A pleasant conceited

black Letter, to which it might have been supposed Sir
John Harrington alluded, had he not spoken of the Dis-
covery as a *new* one, and recommended it as worthy the
notice of his Countrymen: I am persuaded the method
in the old Bard will not be thought *either*. At the end of
the sixth Volume of *Leland*'s *Itinerary*, we are *favoured*
by Mr. *Hearne* with a *Macaronic* Poem on a Battle at
Oxford between the Scholars and the Townsmen ; on a line
of which,

" Invadunt aulas *bycheson cum forth* geminantes,"
our Commentator very wisely and gravely remarks:—
" *Bycheson*, id est, *Son* of a *Byche*, ut è Codice *Rawlinso-
niano* edidi. Eo nempe modo quo et olim *Whorson*
dixerunt pro *Son of a Whore*. Exempla habemus cum
alibi tum in libello quodam lepido & antiquo (inter Codices
Seldenianos in Bibl. *Bodl.*) qui inscribitur: *The Wife
lapped in Morel's Skyn : or the Taming of a Shrew*. Ubi
pag. 36, sic legimus :—

" They wrestled togyther thus they two
So long that the clothes asunder went.
And to the ground he threwe her tho,
That cleane from the backe her smock he rent.
In every hand a rod he gate,
And layd upon her a right good pace:
Asking of her what game was that,
And she cried out, *Horeson*, alas, alas."
Et pag. 42:—
Come downe now in this seller so deepe,
And Morels skin there shall you see :
With many a rod that hath made me to weepe,
When the blood ranne downe fast by my knee.

History, called, *The Taming of a Shrew*—sundry times acted by the Earl of *Pembroke* his Servants." Which seems to have been republished by the Remains of that Company in 1607, when *Shakspeare's* copy appeared at the *Black Friars* or the *Globe.*—Nor let this seem derogatory from the character of our Poet. There is no reason to believe, that he wanted to claim the Play as his own; it was not even printed till some years after his death: but he merely revived it on his Stage as a *Manager.*——*Ravenscroft* assures us, that this was really the case with *Titus Andronicus;* which, it may be observed, hath not *Shakspeare's* name on the Title-page of the only Edition published in his lifetime. Indeed, from every internal mark, I have not the least doubt but this *horrible* Piece was originally written by the Author of the *Lines* thrown into the mouth of the *Player* in *Hamlet,* and of the *Tragedy of Locrine;* which likewise, from some assistance perhaps given to his Friend, hath been unjustly and ignorantly charged upon *Shakspeare.*

But the *Sheet-anchor* holds fast: *Shakspeare* himself hath left some Translations from *Ovid.* The Epistles, says one, of *Paris* and *Helen* give

The Mother this beheld, and cryed out, alas :
And ran out of the seller as she had been wood.
She came to the table where the company was,
And sayd out, *Horeson,* I will see thy harte blood."

a sufficient proof of his accquaintance with *that* poet ; and it may be concluded, says another, that he was a competent judge of *other* Authors, who wrote in the same language.

This hath been the universal cry, from Mr. *Pope* himself to the Criticks of yesterday. Possibly, however, the Getlemen will hesitate a moment, if we tell them, that *Shakspeare* was *not* the Author of these Translations. Let them turn to a forgotten book, by *Thomas Heywood,* called *Britaines Troy,* printed by *W. Jaggard* in 1609, *Fol.,* and they will find these identical Epistles, " which being so pertinent to our Historie, says *Heywood, I* thought necessarie to translate." How then came they ascribed to *Shakspeare ?* We will tell them that likewise. The same voluminous Writer published an *Apology for Actors,* 4to, 1612, and in an Appendix directed to his new Printer, *Nic. Okes,* he accuses his old one, *Jaggard,* of " taking the two Epistles of *Paris* to *Helen,* and *Helen* to *Paris,* and printing them in a less volume under the name of *another ;*—but *he* was much offended with Master *Jaggard,* that, altogether unknowne to him, he had presumed to make so bold with his Name*." In the same work of *Heywood* are

---

* It may seem little matter of wonder, that the name of *Shakspeare* should be borrowed for the benefit of the Bookseller ; and by the way, as probably for a *Play* as a *Poem* :

all the other Translations, which have been printed in the modern Editions of the Poems of *Shakspeare.*

You now hope for land : We have seen through little matters, but what must be done with a whole book ?— In 1751, was reprinted "A compendious or briefe Examination of certayne ordinary Complaints of diuers of our Countrymen in these our Days : which although they are in some parte unjust and friuolous, yet are they all by way of Dialogue throughly debated and discussed by *William Shakspeare,* Gentleman." 8vo.

This extraordinary piece was originally published in 4to, 1581, and dedicated by the Author, "To the most vertuous and learned Lady, his most deare and soveraigne Princesse, *Elizabeth ;* being inforced by her Majesties late and singular clemency in pardoning certayne his unduetifull misdemeanour." And by the modern Editors, to the late King ; as " a Treatise composed by the most extensive and fertile Genius, that ever any age or nation produced."

Here we join issue with the Writers of that

but modern Criticks may be surprised perhaps at the complaint of *John Hall,* that "certayne Chapters of the *Proverbes,* translated by him into *English* metre, 1550, had before been untruely *entituled* to be the doyngs of Mayster *Thomas Sternhold.*"

excellent, tho' very unequal work, the *Biographia Britannica*:* "if, say they, this piece could be

---

* I must however correct a remark in the *Life* of *Spenser,* which is impotently levelled at the first Criticks of the age. It is observed from the correspondence of *Spenser* and *Gabriel Harvey,* that the Plan of the *Fairy Queen* was laid, and part of it executed in 1580, *three* years before the *Gierusalemme Liberata* was printed : "hence appears the impertinence òf all the apologies for his choice of *Ariosto's* manner in preference to *Tasso's !"*

But the fact is not true with respect to *Tasso.* *Manso* and *Niceron* inform us, that his Poem was published, though imperfectly, in 1574 ; and 1 myself can assure the Biographer, that I have met with at least *six* other Editions, preceding his date for its first publication. I suspect that *Baillet* is accountable for this mistake, who in the *Jugemens des Sçavans,* tom. 3, p. 399, mentions no Edition previous to the 4to, *Venice,* 1583.

It is a question of long standing, whether a part of the *Fairy Queen* hath been *lost,* or whether the work was left *unfinished ;* which may effectually be answered by a single quotation. *William Browne* published some Poems in *Fol.* 1616, under the name of *Britannia's Pastorals,* "esteemed *then,* says *Wood,* to be written in a sublime strain, and for subject *amorous* and *very pleasing."*——In one of which, *Book* 2, *Song* 1, he thus speaks of *Spenser:*

" He sung th' heroicke Knights of Faiery land
In lines so elegant, of such command,
That had the *Thracian* plaid but halfe so well,
He had not left *Eurydice* in hell.
But ære he ended his melodious Song,
An host of *Angels* flew the clouds among,

written by our Poet, it would be absolutely decisive in the dispute about his learning; for
many quotations appear in it from the *Greek* and
Latin Classicks."

The concurring circumstances of the *Name*,
and the *Misdeameanor*, which is supposed to be
the old Story of *Deer-stealing*, seem fairly to
challenge our Poet for the Author: but they hesitate.—His claim may appear to be confuted by
the date 1581, when *Shakspeare* was only *Seven-
teen*, and the *long* experience which the Writer
talks of.—But I will not keep you in suspense:
the book was *not* written by *Shakspeare*.

Strype, in his *Annals*, calls the Author SOME
learned Man, and this gave me the first suspicion.
I knew very well, that honest *John* (to use the
language of Sir *Thomas Bodley*) did not waste his
time with such *baggage books* as *Plays* and
Poems ; yet I must suppose that he had *heard*
of the name of *Shakspeare.* After a while I met

> And rapt this Swan from his attentive mates,
> To make him one of their associates
> In heauens faire Quire; where now he sings the praise
> Of Him that is the *First and Last of Dayes*."

It appears, that *Browne* was intimate with *Drayton*,
Jonson, and *Selden*, by their poems prefixed to his Book;
he had therefore good opportunities of being acquainted
with the fact abovementioned. Many of his Poems remain
in MS. We have in our Library at *Emmanuel* a Masque of
his, presented at the Inner Temple, *Jan.* 13, 1614. The
subject is the Story of *Ulysses and Circe.*

M

with the original Edition. Here in the Title-page, and at the end of the Dedication, appear only the Initials, **W. S.** Gent.; and presently I was informed by *Anthony Wood,* that the book in question was written, not by *William Shak-speare,* but by *William Stafford,* Gentleman*; which at once accounted for the *Misdemeanour* in the Dedication. For *Stafford* had been concerned at that time, and was indeed afterward, as *Camden* and the other Annalists inform us, with some of the conspirators against *Elizabeth,* which he properly calls his *unduetifull* behaviour.

I hope, by this time, that any one open to conviction may be nearly satisfied; and I will promise to give you on this head very little more trouble.

The justly celebrated Mr. *Warton* hath favoured us, in his *Life of* Dr. *Bathurst,* with some *hearsay* particulars concerning *Shakspeare* from the papers of *Aubrey,* which had been in the hands of *Wood;* and I ought not to suppress them, as the *last* seems to make against my doctrine. They came originally, I find, on consulting the MS. from one Mr. *Beeston ;* and I am

---

* *Fasti,* 2d Edit. vol. 1, 208.—It will be seen on turning to the former Edition, that the latter part of the Paragraph belongs to another *Stafford.* I have since observed, that *Wood* is not the first who hath given us the true Author of the Pamphlet.

sure Mr. *Warton*, whom I have the honour to call my Friend, and an Associate in the question, will be in no pain about their credit.

" *William Shakspeare*'s Father was a Butcher: while he was a Boy he exercised his Father's trade, but when he killed a Calf, he would do it in a high stile, and make a speech. This *William* being inclined *naturally* to Poetry and Acting, came to *London*, I guess, about *eighteen*, and was an Actor in one of the Playhouses, and did act *exceedingly well*. He began *early* to make Essays in dramatique Poetry.—The humour of the *Constable* in the *Midsummer Night's Dream* he happened to take at *Crendon*** in *Bucks*.—I think I have been told, that he left near three hundred pounds to a *Sister*.—*He understood Latin pretty well*, FOR *he had been in his younger yeares a Schoolmaster in the Country*."

I will be short in my animadversions, and take them in their order.

---

* It was observed in the former Edition, that this place is not met with in *Spelman*'s *Villare*, or in *Adam*'s *Index*; nor, it might have been added, in the *first* and the *last* performance of this sort, *Speed*'s *Tables* and *Whatley*'s *Gazetteer*: perhaps, however, it may be meant under the name of *Crandon*;—but the inquiry is of no importance.— It should, I think, be written *Credendon*; though better Antiquaries than *Aubrey* have acquiesced in the vulgar corruption.

The account of the *Trade* of the Family is not only contrary to all other Tradition, but, as it may seem, to the instrument from the Herald's Office, so frequently reprinted.——*Shakspeare* most certainly went to *London,* and commenced Actor through necessity, not natural inclination. Nor have we any reason to suppose that he did act *exceedingly well.* *Rowe* tells us from the information of *Betterton,* who was inquisitive into this point, and had very early opportunities of Inquiry from Sir *W. Davenant,* that he was no *extraordinary Actor,* and that the top of his performance was the Ghost in his own *Hamlet.* Yet this *Chef d Œuvre* did not please: I will give you an original stroke at it. Dr. *Lodge,* who was for ever pestering the town with Pamphlets, published, in the year 1596, *Wits Miserie, and the Worlds Madnesse, discovering the Devils incarnat of this Age,* 4to. One of these Devils is *Hate-virtue,* or *Sorrow for another mans good successe,* who, says the Doctor, is " *a foule lubber,* and looks as pale as the Visard of the *Ghost,* which cried so miserably at the Theatre, like an Oister-wife, *Hamlet revenge.*" Thus you see Mr. *Holt's* supposed *proof,* in the Appendix to the late Edition, that *Hamlet* was written after 1597, or perhaps 1602, will by no means hold good, whatever might be the case of the particular passage on which it is founded.

Nor does it appear that *Shakspeare* did begin *early* to make *Essays in Dramatique Poetry :* the *Arraignment of Paris,* 1584, which hath so often been ascribed to him on the credit of *Kirkman* and *Winstanley*,* was witten by *George Peele;* and *Shakspeare* is not met with, even as an *Assistant,* till at least seven years afterward†. —*Nash* in his Epistle to the Gentlemen Students of both Universities, prefixed to *Greene's Arcadia,* 4to, *black Letter,* recommends his Friend *Peele,* " as the chiefe supporter of pleasance now living, the *Atlas* of Poetrie, and *primus Verborum artifex;* whose first increase, the *Arraignment of Paris,* might plead to their opinions his pregnant dexteritie of wit, and manifold varietie of inuention‡."

* These people, who were the *Curls* of the last age, ascribe likewise to our Author those miserable Performances, *Mucidorus,* and the *Merry Devil of Edmonton.*

† Mr. *Pope* asserts, " The troublesome Raigne of King *John,*" in 2 parts, 1611, to have been written by *Shakspeare* and *Rowley ;*—which Edition is a mere Copy of another in *black Letter,* 1591. But I find his assertion is somewhat to be doubted :—for the old Edition hath no name of *Author* at all ; and that of 1611 the Initials only, *W. Sh.,* in the Title-page.

‡ *Peele* seems to have been taken into the patronage of the Earl of *Northumberland* about 1593, to whom he dedicates in that year, " *The Honour of the Garter,* a Poem Gratulatorie——the *Firstling* consecrated to his noble name."——" He was esteemed," says *Anthony Wood,* " a

In the next place, unfortunately, there is neither such a Character as a *Constable* in the *Midsummer Night's Dream ;* nor was the *three hundred pounds* Legacy to a Sister, but a Daughter.

And to close the whole, it is not possible, ac-

most noted Poet, 1579 ; but when or where he died, I cannot tell; for *so it is,* and always *hath been,* that most POETS die *poor,* and consequently obscurely, and a hard matter it is to trace them to their Graves. *Claruit* 1599."—*Ath. Oxon.* vol. 1, p. 300.

We had lately in a periodical Pamphlet, called, *The Theatrical Review,* a very *curious* Letter under the name of *George Peele,* to one Master *Henrie Marle ;* relative to a dispute between *Shakspeare* and *Alleyn,* which was compromised by *Ben Jonson.*——" I never longed for thy companye more than last night ; we were all verie merrie at the *Globe,* when *Ned Alleyn* did not scruple to affyrme pleasauntly to thy friende *Will,* that he had stolen hys speeche about the excellencie of acting in *Hamlet* hys Tragedye, from conversaytions manifold, whych had passed between them, and opinions gyven by *Alleyn* touchyng that subjecte. *Shakspeare* did not take this talk in good sorte ; but *Jonson* did put an end to the stryfe wyth wittielie saying, thys affaire needeth no contentione : you stole it from *Ned* no doubte : do not marvel : haue you not seene hym acte tymes out of number ?"——This is pretended to be printed from the original MS. dated 1600 ; which agrees well enough with *Wood's Claruit:* but, unluckily, *Peele* was dead at least two years before. " As *Anacreon* died by the *Pot,*" says *Meres,* " so *George Peele* by the *Pox.*" *Wit's Treasury,* 1598, p. 286.

cording to *Aubrey* himself, that *Shakspeare* could have been some *years a Schoolmaster in the Country;* on which circumstance only the supposition of his learning is professedly founded. He was not surely *very* young when he was employed to *kill Calves,* and he commenced Player about *Eighteen !*—The truth is, that he left his Father, for a Wife, a year sooner ; and had at least two Children born at *Stratford* before he retired from thence to *London.* It is therefore sufficiently clear, that poor *Anthony* had too much reason for his character of *Aubrey :* you will find it in his own Account of his Life, published by *Hearne,* which I would earnestly recommend to any Hypochondriack :

" A pretender to Antiquities, roving, magotie-headed, and sometimes little better than crased : and being exceedingly credulous, would stuff his many Letters sent to A. W. with *folliries* and misinformations," p. 577.

Thus much for the Learning of *Shakspeare* with respect to the ancient languages : indulge me with an observation or two on his supposed knowledge of the modern ones, and I will promise to release you.

" It is *evident,* we have been told, that he was not unacquainted with the *Italian ;*" but let us inquire into the *Evidence.*

Certainly some *Italian* words and phrases appear in the Works of *Shakspeare*; yet if we had nothing else to observe, their Orthography might lead us to suspect them to be not of the *writer's* importation.　But we can go further, and prove this.

When *Pistol* "chears up himself with ends of verse," he is only a copy of *Hanniball Gonsaga,* who ranted on yielding himself a Prisoner to an *English* Captain in the *Low Countries,* as you may read in an old Collection of Tales, called *Wits, Fits, and Fancies*,*

" Si Fortuna me tormenta,
Ill speranza me contenta."

And Sir *Richard Hawkins,* in his Voyage to the South Sea, 1593, throws out the same jingling Distich on the loss of his Pinnace :—

"Master *Page,* sit; good Master *Page,* sit ; *Proface.*　What you want in meat, we'll have in drink," says Justice *Shallow's Fac totum, Davy,* in the 2d Part of *Henry* IV.

Proface, Sir *Thomas Hanmer* observes to be *Italian,* from *profaccia, much good may it do you.*　Mr. *Johnson* rather thinks it a mistake for

---

* By one *Anthony Copley,* 4to, *black Letter :* it seems to have had many Editions; perhaps the last was in 1614.— The first piece of this sort, that I have met with, was printed by *T. Berthelet,* though not mentioned by *Ames,* called, " Tales, and quicke Answeres very mery and pleasant to rede." 4to, no date.

perforce. Sir *Thomas* however is right; yet it is no argument for his Author's *Italian* knowledge.

Old *Heywood,* the Epigrammatist, addressed his Readers long before,

" Readers, reade this thus : for Preface, *Proface,*
Much good do it you, the poore repast here," &c.

Woorkes, Lond. 4to, 1562.

And *Dekker* in his Play, *If it be not good, the Diuel is in it,* (which is certainly true, for it is full of Devils) makes *Shackle-soule,* in the character of *Friar Rush,* tempt his Brethren with " choice of dishes"

" To which *proface ;* with blythe lookes sit yee."

Nor hath it escaped the quibbling manner of the *Water-poet,* in the title of a Poem prefixed to his *Praise of Hempseed,* " A Preamble, Preatrot, Preagallop, Preapace, or Preface ; and *Proface,* my Masters, if your Stomacks serve."

But the Editors are not contented without coining *Italian.* " *Rivo, says the Drunkard,*" is an expression of the *madcap* prince of *Wales ;* which Sir *Thomas Hanmer* corrects to *Ribi, Drink away,* or *again,* as it should rather be translated. Dr. *Warburton* accedes to this, and Mr. *Johnson* hath admitted it into his Text ; but with an observation, that *Rivo* might possibly be the cant of *English* Taverns. And so indeed it was : it occurs frequently in *Marston.* Take a quotation from his Comedy of *What you will,* 1607 :

N

" Musicke, Tobacco, Sacke, and Sleepe,
The Tide of Sorrow backward keep:
If thou art sad at others fate,
Rivo drink deep, give care the mate."

In *Love's Labour Lost, Boyet* calls Don *Armado*,
———" A Spaniard that keeps here in Court,
A Phantasme, a *Monarcho*."——

Here too Sir *Thomas* is willing to palm *Italian* upon us. We should read, it seems, *Mammuccio*, a Mammet, or Puppet : Ital. *Mammuccia*. But the allusion is to a fantastical *Character* of the time.—" Popular applause," says *Meres*, " dooth nourish some, neither do they gape after any other thing, but vaine praise and glorie,— as in our age *Peter Shakerlye* of *Paules*, and MONARCHO that liued about the Court." P. 178.

I fancy you will be satisfied with one more instance :

" *Baccare*, You are marvellous forward, quoth *Gremio* to *Petruchio* in the *Taming of the Shrew*.

" But not so *forward,* says Mr. *Theobald*, as our Editors are *indolent*. This is a stupied corruption of the press, that none of them have dived into. We must read *Baccalare,* as Mr. *Warburton* acutely observed to me, by which the *Italians* mean, Thou ignorant, presumptuous Man."—" Properly indeed," adds Mr. *Heath*, " a *graduated* Scholar, but ironically and sarcastically, a *pretender* to Scholarship."

This is admitted by the Editors and Criticks of

every Denomination. Yet the word is neither
wrong, nor *Italian :* it was an old proverbial one,
used frequently by *John Heywood,* who hath
made, what he pleases to call, *Epigrams* upon it.
Take two of them, such as they are.

> " *Backare,* quoth *Mortimer* to his Sow :
> Went that Sow *backe* at that biddyng trowe you ?"
>
> " *Backare,* quoth *Mortimer* to his sow ; se
> *Mortimers* sow speakth as good *latin* as he."

Howel takes this from *Heywood,* in his *Old
Sawes and Adages :* and *Philpot* introduces it
into the Proverbs collected by *Camden.*

We have but few observations concerning
Shakspeare's knowledge of the *Spanish* tongue.
Dr. *Grey* indeed is willing to suppose, that the
Plot of *Romeo and Juliet* may be borrowed
from a Comedy of *Lopes de Vega.* But the
Spaniard, who was certainly acquainted with
Bandello, hath not only changed the Catastrophe,
but the names of the Characters.   Neither *Romeo*
nor *Juliet,* neither *Montague* nor *Capulet,* appears in this performance : and how came they
to the knowledge of *Shakspeare ?*—Nothing is
more certain, than that he chiefly followed the
Translation by *Painter* from the *French* of *Bois-
teau,* and hence arise the Deviations from *Bandello's* original *Italian*.*   It seems however from

---

* It is remarked, that " *Paris,* though in one place called
Earl, is most commonly styled the *Countie* in this Play.

a passage in *Ames's* Typographical Antiquities, that *Painter* was not the only Translator of this popular Story; and it is possible, therefore, that *Shakspeare* might have other assistance.

In the Induction to the *Taming of the Shrew*, the Tinker attempts to talk *Spanish;* and *consequently* the Author himself was acquainted with it.

"*Paucus pallabris,* let the World slide, *Sessa.*"

But this is a burlesque on *Hieronymo;* the piece

Shakspeare seems to have preferred, for some reason or other, the *Italian Conte* to our *Count:*—perhaps he took it from the old *English* Novel from which he is said to have taken his Plot."—He certainly did so : *Paris* is there first styled a *young Earle,* and afterward *Counte, Countee,* and *County;* according to the unsettled Orthography of the time.

The word however is frequently met with in other Writers; particularly in *Fairfax :*

"As when a Captaine doth besiege some hold,

  Set in a marish or high on a hill,

And trieth waies and wiles a thousand fold,

  To bring the piece subjected to his will ;

So far'd the *Countie* with the Pagan bold," &c.

Godfrey of Bulloigne, Book 7, st. 90.

"*Fairfax,*" says Mr. Hume, "hath translated *Tasso* with an elegance and ease, and at the same time with an exactness, which for that age are surprising. Each line in the original is faithfully rendered by a correspondent line in the translation." The former part of this character is extremely true, but the latter not quite so. In the *Book* above-quoted *Tasso* and *Fairfax* do not even agree in the Number of *Stanzas.*

of Bombast, that I have mentioned to you before :

"What new device have they devised, trow?
Pocas pallabras," &c.————

Mr. *Whalley* tells us, "the Author of this piece hath the happiness to be at this time unknown, the remembrance of him having perished with himself:" *Philips* and others ascribe it to one *William Smith;* but I take this opportunity of informing him, that it was written by *Thomas Kyd;* if he will accept the authority of his contemporary, *Heywood.*

More hath been said concerning *Shakspeare*'s acquaintance with the *French* language. In the Play of *Henry the Fifth,* we have a whole Scene in it, and in other places it occurs familiarly in the Dialogue.

We may observe in general, that the early Editions have not half the quantity; and every sentence, or rather every word, most ridiculously blundered. These, for several reasons, could not possibly be published by the Author*; and it

* Every writer on *Shakspeare* hath expressed his asto-nishment, that his author was not solicitous to secure his Fame by a correct Edition of his performances. This matter is not understood. When a Poet was connected with a particular Playhouse, he constantly sold his Works to the *Company,* and it was their interest to keep them from a number of Rivals. A favourite Piece, as *Heywood* informs us, only got into print, when it was copied *by the ear,*

is extremely probable that the *French* ribaldry
was at first inserted by a different hand, as the

" for a double sale would bring on a suspicion of honestie."
Shakspeare therefore himself published nothing in the
Drama : when he left the Stage, his copies remained with
his Fellow-Managers, *Heminge* and *Condell ;* who at their
own retirement, about seven years after the death of their
Author, gave the World the Edition now known by the
name of the *first Folio ;* and call the previous publications,
" stolne and surreptitious, maimed and deformed by the
frauds and stealths of injurious impostors." But *this* was
printed from the Playhouse Copies ; which in a series of
years had been frequently altered, through convenience,
caprice, or ignorance.   We have a sufficient instance of
the liberties taken by the Actors, in an old pamphlet by
Nash, called *Lenten Stuffe, with the Prayse of the red
Herring,* 4to, 1599, where he assures us, that in a Play of
his, called the *Isle of Dogs,* " *foure acts,* without his consent, or the least guesse of his drift or scope, were supplied
by the Players."
    This however was not his first quarrel with them.   In
the Epistle prefixed to *Greene's Arcadia,* which I have
quoted before, *Tom.* hath a lash at some " vaine glorious
Tragedians," and very plainly at *Shakspeare* in particular ;
which will serve for an answer to an observation of Mr.
Pope, that had almost been forgotten :   " It was thought a
praise to *Shakspeare,* that he scarce ever blotted a line :—
I believe the common opinion of his want of learning pro-
ceeded from no better ground.   This too might be thought
a *praise* by some."——But hear *Nash,* who was far from
praising :   " I leaue all these to the mercy of their
Mother-tongue, that feed on nought but the crums that
fall from the *Translator's* trencher.·——That could scarcely

many additions most certainly were after he had
left the Stage.——Indeed, every friend to his
memory will not easily believe, that he was acquainted with the Scene between *Catharine* and
the *old Gentlewoman ;* or surely he would not
have admitted such obscenity and nonsense.

Latinize their neck verse if they should haue neede, yet
English Seneca read by Candlelight yeelds many good
sentences——hee will affoord you whole *Hamlets,* I should
say, *Handfuls* of tragicall speeches."—I cannot determine
exactly when this *Epistle* was first published ; but I fancy
it will carry the original *Hamlet* somewhat further back
than we have hitherto done : and it may be observed, that
the oldest Copy now extant is said to be " Enlarged to
almost as much againe as it was." *Gabriel Harvey* printed,
at the end of the year 1592, " Foure Letters and certaine
Sonnetts, especially touching *Robert Greene,*" in one of
which his *Arcadia* is mentioned. Now *Nash's* Epistle must
have been previous to these, as *Gabriel* is quoted in it with
applause ; and the *Foure Letters* were the beginning of a
quarrel. *Nash* replied, in " Strange Newes of the inter-
cepting certaine Letters, and a Convoy of Verses, as they
were going *privilie* to victuall the *Low Countries,* 1593."
Harvey rejoined the same year in " *Pierce's* Supererogation,
or a new Praise of the old Asse." And *Nash* again, in
" Have with you to *Saffron-walden,* or *Gabriell Harvey's*
Hunt is up; containing a full Answer to the eldest Sonne of
the Halter-maker, 1596."

Dr. *Lodge* calls *Nash* our *true English Aretine ;* and
John Taylor, in his *Kicksey Winsey, or a Lerry Come-twang*,
even makes an oath " by sweet Satyricke *Nash* his urne."—
He died before 1606, as appears from an old Comedy, called
"The Return from *Parnassus.*"

Mr. *Hawkins,* in the Appendix to Mr. *John-son*'s Edition, hath an ingenious observation to prove, that *Shakspeare,* supposing the *French* to be his, had very little knowledge of the language:

" Est-il impossible d'eschapper la force de ton *Bras?*" says a *Frenchman.*—" *Brass,* cur?" replies *Pistol.*

" Almost any one knows that the French word *Bras* is pronounced *Brau ;* and what resemblance of sound does this bear to *Brass ?*"

Mr. *Johnson* makes a doubt, whether the pronunciation of the French language may not be changed since *Shakspeare*'s time, " if not," says he, " it may be suspected that some other man wrote the *French* scenes:" but this does not appear to be the case, at least in this termination, from the rules of the Grammarians, or the practice of the Poets. I am certain of the former from the *French Alphabeth* of *De la Mothe*,* and the *Orthoepia Gallica* of *John Eliot†;* and of the

---

* *Lond.* 1592, 8vo.

† *Lond.* 1593, 4to. *Eliot* is almost the only *witty* Grammarian that I have had the fortune to meet with. In his Epistle prefatory to the *Gentle Doctors of Gaule,* he cries out for persecution, very like *Jack* in that most poignant of Satires, the *Tale of a Tub,* " I pray you be readie quickly to cauill at my booke, I beseech you heartily calumniate my doings with speede, I request you humbly controll my method as soone as you may, I earnestly entreat you hisse at my inventions," &c.

latter from the Rhymes of *Marot, Ronsard,* and
Du Bartas. Connections of this kind were very
common. *Shakspeare* himself assisted *Ben
Jonson* in his *Sejanus,* as it was originally
written; and *Fletcher* in his *Two noble Kinsmen.*

But what if the *French* scene were occasionally introduced into every Play on this subject ? and perhaps there were more than one
before our Poet's.—In *Pierce Penilesse his Sup-
plication to the Diuell,* 4to, 1592 (which, it
seems, from the Epistle to the Printer, was not
the first Edition), the Author, *Nash,* exclaims,
" What a glorious thing it is to have *Henry the
Fifth* represented on the Stage leading the *French
King* prisoner, and forcing both him and the
Dolphin to sweare fealty !"—And it appears from
the Jests of the famous Comedian, *Tarlton,* 4to,
1611, that he had been particularly celebrated
in the Part of the *Clown* in *Henry the Fifth ;* but
no such Character exists in the Play of *Shakspeare.*——*Henry the Sixth* hath ever been
doubted ; and a passage in the above-quoted piece
of *Nash* may give us reason to believe, it was
previous to our Author. " How would it haue
joyed braue *Talbot* (the terror of the *French*) to
thinke that after he had lyen two hundred yeare
in his Toomb, he should triumph again on the
Stage; and haue his bones new embalmed with
the teares of ten thousand spectators at least (at

O

seuerall times), who in the Tragedian that repre-
sents his person, imagine they behold him fresh
bleeding."——I have no doubt but *Henry the
Sixth* had the same Author with *Edward the
Third*, which hath been recovered to the world in
Mr. *Capell's Prolusions.*

It hath been observed, that the *Giant of Rabe-
lais* is sometimes alluded to by *Shakspeare ;* and in
his time no translation was extant. But the story
was in every one's hand.

In a Letter by one *Laneham,* or *Langham,* for
the name is written differently*, concerning the
entertainment at *Killingwoorth Castle,* printed
1575, we have a list of the vulgar Romances of
the age, "King *Arthurz* book, *Huon* of *Bur-
deaus,* Friar *Rous, Howleglass,* and GARGANTUA.
Meres† mentions him as equally hurtful to

* It is indeed of no importance ; but I suspect the
former to be right, as I find it corrupted afterward to *Lanam*
and *Lanum.*

† This Author, by a pleasant mistake in some sensible
Conjectures on Shakspeare lately printed at *Oxford,* is
quoted by the name of *Maister.* Perhaps the Title-page
was imperfect ; it runs thus, " Palladis Tamia. Wits Treasury. Being the second Part of Wits Commonwealth, by
Francis Meres Maister of Artes of both Universities."

I am glad out of gratitude to this man, who hath been of
frequent service to me, that I am enabled to perfect *Wood*'s
account of him, from the assistance of our *Master*'s very
accurate List of Graduates (which it would do honour to

young minds with the *Four Sons* of *Aymon,* and
the *Seven Champions.* And *John Taylor* hath
him likewise in his catalogue of *Authors,* prefixed
to Sir *Gregory Nonsence*.*

But, to come to a conclusion, I will give you an
irrefragable argument, that *Shakspeare* did *not*
understand *two* very common words in the *French*
and *Latin* languages.

According to the articles of agreement between
the Conqueror *Henry* and the King of *France,*
the latter was to style the former (in the corrected

the University to print at the publick expense) and the kind
information of a Friend from the Register of his Parish :—
He was originally of *Pembroke-Hall,* B.A. in 1587, and
M.A. 1591. About 1602 he became Rector of *Wing* in
Rutland; and died there, 1646, in the 81st year of his age.

* I have quoted many pieces of *John Taylor,* but it was
impossible to give their original dates. He may be traced
as an Author for more than half a Century. His *Works*
were collected in *Folio,* 1630, but many were printed
afterward; I will mention one for the Humour of the Title.
"Drinke and welcome, or the famous History of the most
Part of Drinkes in use in *Greate Britain* and *Ireland;* with
an especial Declaration of the Potency, Vertue, and Opera-
tion of our *English* Ale : with a Description of all Sorts of
Waters, from the *Ocean Sea* to the *Tears of a Woman.* 4to,
1633."——In *Wits Merriment, or Lusty Drollery,* 1656,
we have an "Epitaph on *John Taylor,* who was born in the
City of *Glocester,* and dyed in *Phœnix Alley,* in the 75
yeare of his age : you may find him, if the worms have not
devoured him, in *Covent Garden* Church-yard," p. 130.—
He died about two years before.

French of the modern Editions,) " Nostre *tres cher* filz *Henry* Roy d'*Angleterre* ; and in *Latin,* *Prœclarissimus* Filius," &c. What, says Dr. *Warburton,* is *tres cher* in *French, prœclarissimus* in *Latin !* we should read *prœcarissimus.*— This appears to be exceedingly true; but how came the blunder ? it is a typographical one in *Holingshed,* which *Shakspeare* copied ; but must indisputably have corrected, had he been acquainted with the languages.—" Our said Father, during his life, shall name, call, and write us in *French* in this manner : Nostre *tres chier* filz, *Henry* Roy d'*Engleterre*—and in *Latine* in this manner, *Prœclarissimus* filius noster." Edit. 1587, p. 574.

To corroborate this instance, let me observe to you, though it be nothing further to the purpose, that another error of the same kind hath been the source of a mistake in an historical passage of our Author, which hath ridiculously troubled the Criticks.

Richard the Third* harangues his army before the Battle of *Bosworth,*

---

* Some inquiry hath been made for the first Performers of the capital Characters in *Shakspeare.*

We learn, that *Burbage,* the *alter Roscius* of *Camden,* was the original *Richard,* from a passage in the Poems of Bishop *Corbet ;* who introduces his Host at *Bosworth* describing the Battle ;

" Remember whom ye are to cope withal,
A sort of vagabonds, of rascals, runaways—
And who doth lead them but a paltry fellow
Long kept in *Britaine* at *our Mother*'s cost,
A milksop," &c.——

" *Our* Mother," Mr. *Theobald* perceives to be wrong, and *Henry* was somewhere secreted on the *Continent:* he reads therefore, and all the Editors after him,

"Long kept in *Bretagne* at *his* mother's cost."

But give me leave to transcribe a few more lines from *Holingshed,* and you will find at once that *Shakspeare* had been there before ˉme:——" Ye

" But when he would have said King *Richard* died,
And call'd *a Horse, a Horse,* he *Burbage* cried."

The Play on this subject mentioned by Sir *John Harrington* in his *Apologie for Poetrie,* 1591, and sometimes mistaken for *Shakspeare's,* was a *Latin* one, written by Dr. *Legge;* and acted at *St. John's* in our University, some years before 1588, the date of the Copy in the *Museum.* This appears from a better MS. in our Library at *Emmanuel,* with the names of the original Performers.

It is evident from a passage in *Camden's Annals,* that there was an old Play likewise on the subject of *Richard the Second,* but I know not in what language. Sir *Gelley Merrick,* who was concerned in the harebrained business of the Earl of *Essex,* and was hanged for it with the ingenious *Cuffe* in 1601, is accused amongst other things, " quod *exoletam* Tragœdiam de tragicâ abdicatione Regis *Ricardi secundi* in publico Theatro coram Conjuratis datâ pecuniâ agi curasset."

see further, how a companie of traitors, theeves, outlaws and runnagates be aiders and partakers of his feat and enterprise.—And to begin with the erle of Richmond captaine of this rebellion, he is a Welsh milksop—brought up by *my Moother's* meanes and mine, like a captive in a close cage in the court of *Francis* duke of *Britaine.*" p. 756.

Holingshed copies this *verbatim* from his brother Chronicler *Hall,* Edit. 1548, *fol.* 54; but his Printer hath given us by accident the word *Moother* instead of *Brother,* as it is in the original, and ought to be in *Shakspeare**.

I hope, my good Friend, you have by this time acquitted our great Poet of all piratical depredations on the Ancients, and are ready to receive my *conclusion.* He remembered perhaps enough

---

* I cannot take my leave of *Holingshed* without clearing up a difficulty, which hath puzzled his Biographers. *Nicholson* and other Writers have *supposed* him a *Clergyman.* *Tanner* goes further, and tells us, that he was educated at *Cambridge,* and actually took the degree of M.A. in 1544.——Yet it appears by his Will, printed by *Hearne,* that at the end of life he was only a *Steward* or a *Servant* in some capacity or other, to *Thomas Burdett,* Esq. of *Bromcote* in *Warwickshire.*—These things Dr. *Campbell* could not reconcile. The truth is, we have no claim to the education of the *Chronicler:* the M.A. in 1544 was not *Raphael,* but one *Ottiwell Holingshed,* who was afterward named by the founder one of the first Fellows of *Trinity College.*

of his *school-boy* learning to put the *Hig, hag, hog,* into the mouth of Sir *Hugh Evans;* and might pick up in the Writers of the time*, or the course of his conversation, a familiar phrase or two of *French* or *Italian ;* but his *Studies* were most demonstratively confined to *Nature* and *his own Language.*

In the course of this disquisition, you have often smiled at " all such reading as was never read ;" and possibly I may have indulged it too far : but it is the reading necessary for a comment on *Shakspeare.* Those who apply solely to the Ancients for this purpose, may with equal wisdom study the TALMUD for an Exposition of TRISTRAM SHANDY. Nothing but an intimate acquaintance with the Writers of the time, who are frequently of no other value, can point out his allusions, and ascertain his phraseology. The

---

* *Ascham* in the Epistle prefixed to his *Toxophilus,* 1571, observes of them, that " Manye *Englishe* writers, usinge straunge wordes, as *Lattine, Frenche,* and *Italian,* do make all thinges darke and harde. Ones, says he, I communed with a man which reasoned the *Englishe* tongue to be enriched and encreased thereby, sayinge, Who will not prayse that feast, where a man shall drincke at a dinner both wyne, ale, and beere ? Truly (quoth I) they be al good, euery one taken by himselfe alone ; but if you put Malmesye and sacke, redde wyne and white, ale and beere, and al in one pot, you shall make a drinke neither easye to be knowen, nor yet holsome for the bodye."

Reformers of his Text are for ever equally positive, and equally wrong. The cant of the age, a
provincial expression, an obscure proverb, an
obsolete custom, a hint at a person or a fact no
longer remembered, hath continually defeated the
best of our *Guessers:* you must not suppose
me to speak at random, when I assure you, that,
from some forgotten book or other, I can demonstrate this to you in many hundred places ; and
I almost wish that I had not been persuaded into
a different employment.

　　Though I have as much of the *NataleSolum**
about me as any man whatsoever, yet I own the
Primrose Path is still more pleasing than the
Fosse or the *Watling Street:*

　　　" Age cannot wither it, nor custom stale
　　　Its infinite variety."———

And when I am fairly rid of the dust of topo-
graphical Antiquity, which hath continued much
longer about me than I expected, you may very
probably be troubled again with the ever fruitful
subject of SHAKSPEARE and his COMMENTATORS.

　　* This alludes to an intended Publication of the
Antiquities of the Town of Leicester. The Work was just
begun at the Press, when the Writer was called to the
principal tuition of a large College, and was obliged to
decline the undertaking. The plates, however, and some
of the materials, have been long ago put into the hands of
a Gentleman who is every way qualified to make a proper
use of them.

APPENDIX

TO

MR. COLMAN'S TRANSLATION OF TERENCE.

(OCTAVO EDITION.)

THE reverend and ingenious Mr. *Farmer*, in his curious and entertaining *Essay on the Learning of Shakspeare*, having done me the honour to animadvert on some passages in the preface to this translation, I cannot dismiss this edition without declaring how far I coincide with that gentleman; although what I then threw out carelessly on the subject of this pamphlet was merely incidental, nor did I mean to enter the lists as a champion to defend either side of the question.

It is most true, as Mr. *Farmer* takes for granted, that I had never met with the old comedy called *The Supposes*, nor has it ever yet fallen into my hands; yet I am willing to grant, on Mr. *Farmer*'s authority, that *Shakspeare* borrowed part of the plot of *The Taming of the Shrew* from that old translation of *Ariosto*'s play by *George Gascoign*, and had no obligations to *Plautus*. I will accede also to the truth of Dr. *Johnson*'s and Mr. *Farmer*'s observation, that

P

the line from *Terence,* exactly as it stands in
Shakspeare, is extant in *Lilly* and *Udall's Floures
for Latin Speaking.*   Still, however, *Shakspeare*'s
total ignorance of the learned languages remains
to be proved; for it must be granted, that such
books are put into the hands of those who are
learning those languages, in which class we
must necessarily rank *Shakspeare,* or he could
not even have quoted *Terence* from *Udall* or
Lilly; nor is it likely that so rapid a genius
should not have made some further progress.
" Our author," says Dr. *Johnson,* as quoted by
Mr. *Farmer,* " had this line from *Lilly;* which
I mention, that it may not be brought as an
argument of his learning."   It is, however, an
argument that he read *Lilly;* and a few pages
further it seems pretty certain that the author of
The Taming of the Shrew had at least read
Ovid, from whose Epistle we find these lines :

> " Hàc ibat Simois; hic est Sigeïa tellus;
> " Hic steterat Priami regia celsa senis."

And what does Dr. *Johnson* say on this occasion?
Nothing.   And what does Mr. *Farmer* say on
this occasion ?   Nothing.

In *Love's Labour's Lost,* which, bad as it is,
is ascribed by Dr. *Johnson* himself to *Shakspeare,*
there occurs the word *thrasonical ;* another argument which seems to shew that he was not unacquainted with the comedies of *Terence;* not to

mention, that the character of the schoolmaster in the same play could not possibly be written by a man who had travelled no further in Latin than *hic, hœc, hoc.*

In *Henry the Sixth* we meet with a quotation from *Virgil:*

"Tantæne animis cœlestibus iræ?"

But this, it seems, proves nothing, any more than the lines from *Terence* and *Ovid*, in *The Taming of the Shrew*; for Mr. *Farmer* looks on *Shakspeare's* property in the comedy to be extremely disputable; and he has no doubt but *Henry the Sixth* had the same author with *Edward the Third*, which had been recovered to the world in Mr. *Capell's* Prolusions.

If any play in the collection bears internal evidence of *Shakspeare's* hand, we may fairly give him *Timon of Athens*. In this play we have a familiar quotation from *Horace :*

"Ira furor brevis est."

I will not maintain but this hemistich may be found in *Lilly* or *Udall*; or that it is not in the *Palace of Pleasure*, or the *English Plutarch*; or that it was not originally foisted in by the players: it stands, however, in the play of *Timon of Athens*.

The world in general, and those who purpose to comment on *Shakspeare* in particular, will owe much to Mr. *Farmer*, whose researches into our old authors throw a lustre on many passages, the obscurity of which must else have been impenetrable. No future *Upton* or *Gildon* will go further than *North*'s translation for *Shakspeare*'s acquaintance with *Plutarch*, or balance between *Dares Phrygius* and *The Troye Booke of Lydgate*. *The Hystorie of Hamblet*, in *black letter*, will for ever supersede *Saxo Grammaticus*; translated novels and ballads will, perhaps, be allowed the sources of *Romeo*, *Lear*, and *The Merchant of Venice*; and *Shakspeare* himself, however unlike *Bayes* in other particulars, will stand convicted of having *transversed* the prose of *Holinshed*; and, at the same time, to prove " that his *studies* lay in his own language," the translations of *Ovid* are determined to be the production of *Heywood*.

" That his *studies* were most demonstratively confined to *nature*, and his *own language*," I readily allow ; but does it hence follow that he was so deplorably ignorant of every other tongue, living or dead, that he only " remembered, perhaps, enough of his *school-boy* learning to put the *hig, hag, hog*, into the mouth of Sir *H. Evans*; and might pick up in the writers of the time, or the course of his conversation, a familiar phrase or two of French or Italian ?" In *Shakspeare*'s plays both these last languages are plentifully scattered ; but, then, we are told they might be impertinent additions of the players. Undoubtedly they might : but there they are, and, perhaps, few of the players had much more learning than *Shakspeare.*

Mr. *Farmer* himself will allow that *Shakspeare* began to learn Latin : I will allow that his *studies* lay in English : but why insist that he neither made any progress at school, nor improved his acquisitions there? The general encomiums of *Suckling, Denham, Milton,* &c. on his *native genius**, prove nothing ; and *Ben Jonson*'s celebrated charge of *Shakspeare*'s *small Latin, and less Greek*†, seems absolutely to decide that he

---

* Mr. *Farmer* closes the general testimonies of *Shakspeare*'s having been only indebted to nature, by saying, "He came out of her hand, *as some one else expresses it,* like *Pallas* out of *Jove*'s head, at full growth and mature." It is whimsical enough, that this *some one else,* whose expression is here quoted to countenance the general notion of *Shakspeare*'s want of literature, should be no other than myself. Mr. *Farmer* does not choose to mention where he met with the expression of *some one else ;* and *some one else* does not choose to mention where he dropt it. *(a)*

† In defence of the various reading of this passage, given in the Preface to the last edition of *Shakspeare,* "small Latin and *no* Greek," Mr. *Farmer* tells us, that "it was adopted above a century ago by *W. Towers,* in a panegyrick on Cartwright." Surely, *Towers* having said that *Cartwright* had *no* Greek, is no proof that *Ben Jonson* said so of *Shakspeare.*

(a) It will appear still more whimsical that this *some one else,* whose

had *some* knowledge of both; and if we may judge by our own time, a man, who has any Greek, is seldom without a very competent share of Latin; and yet such a man is very likely to study *Plutarch* in English, and to read translations of *Ovid*.

See Dr. Farmer's reply to these remarks by Mr. Colman, in a note on LOVE'S LABOUR'S LOST, *vol. vii, p.* 258.

expression is here quoted, may have his claim to it superseded by that of the late Dr. *Young*, who in his *Conjectures on Original Composition* (p. 100, vol. v, edit. 1773) has the following sentence : " An adult genius comes out of nature's hands, as *Pallas* out of *Jove's* head, at full growth and mature. *Shakspeare's* genius was of this kind." Where *some one else* the *first* may have intermediately dropped the contested expression I cannot ascertain; but *some one else* the *second* transcribed it from the author already mentioned.—ANON.

DR. FARMER'S REPLY

TO

MR. COLMAN'S REMARKS.

===

THE use of the word *thrasonical,* in the play of *Love's Labour's Lost* [Act. iv, sc. ii] is no argument that the author had read *Terence :* it was introduced to our language long before *Shakspeare*'s time. *Stanyhurst* writes in a translation of one of Sir *Thomas More*'s epigrams :

" Lynckte was in wedlocke a lofty *thrasonical* hufsnuffe*.

It can scarcely be necessary to animadvert any further upon what **Mr.** *Colman* has advanced in the appendix to his *Terence.* If this gentleman, at his leisure from modern plays, will condescend to open a few old ones, he will soon be satisfied that *Shakspeare* was obliged to learn and repeat, in the course of his profession, such Latin *frag-*

---

* In support of **Dr.** *Farmer*'s opinion, the following passage from *Orlando Furioso,* 1594, may be brought :

" — Knowing him to be a *Thrasonical* mad cap, they have sent me a *Gnathonical* companion," &c.

Greene, in the dedication to his *Arcadia,* has the same word :

" — as of some *thrasonical huffe-snuffe.*"

STEEVENS.

ments as are met with in his works. The formidable one, *ira furor brevis est,* which is quoted from *Timon,* may be found, not in plays only, but in every *critical* essay, from that of King *James* to that of Dean *Swift* inclusive. I will only add, that if Mr. *Colman* had previously looked at the panegyric on *Cartwright,* he would not so strangely have misrepresented my argument from it; but thus it must ever be with the most ingenious men, when they talk *without-book.* Let me, however, take this opportunity of acknowledging the very genteel language which he has been pleased to use on this occasion.

F I N I S.

J. Compton, Printer, Middle Street, Cloth Fair.